I0023258

Homeland Security Operations & Change

SYSTEMOPS™ MODELS

The D&S™ SystemOps™ Models monograph series employs graphic models to describe how complex systems and processes do or could operate. The models provide structured pictures intended to generate common mental models used as frameworks for visualization, communication, analysis and decision.

The series is published by Downey & Small Associates, Inc., System Operations Analysis and Publishing. Suggestions for model topics or improvements to current models can be sent to Editor@SystemOps.com™.

Homeland Security Operations & Change

—

A Framework for Human Resources Management

Albert W. Small, Ph.D.

Elizabeth A. Downey

With Foreword by Pete Smith

Third Edition

Downey & Small Associates, Inc.
System Operations Analysis and Publishing

Downey & Small Associates, Inc., System Operations Analysis and Publishing, Kensington, Maryland, U.S.A., SystemOps@DowneySmall.com™.

Copyright © 2003, 2004, 2011 by Downey & Small Associates, Inc. All rights reserved.
First edition excerpts published in DHS/OPM public meeting 2003
Second edition published 2004
Third edition published 2011

Printed in the United States of America

2015 14 13 12 11   9 8 7 6 5 4 3 2 1

ISBN10: 0-9764580-2-0
ISBN13: 978-0-9764580-2-9

D&S SystemOps™ Model DHS-HRMS Version 2.0

Trademarks: D&S, SystemOps, SystemOps@DowneySmall.com, and SystemOps.com are trademarks of Downey & Small Associates, Inc.

LEGAL NOTICE: This document represents the views of the authors; accuracy and completeness are not guaranteed. Users of this document agree to hold harmless and defend the authors and publisher against claims arising from users' use or transfer of information from this document.

With gratitude to all who sacrifice for our security.

Contents

Diagrams   viii

Figures   viii

Tables   viii

Foreword   ix

Preface   xi

I.   Introduction   1
     Background   1
     Human Resources Management   1
     Operations & Change—Context for Human Resources Management   2
     Need for Graphic Model   3
     Graphic Language   4
     Presentation   4

II. The Operations & Change Model   5
     A0, Operate & Change the Homeland Security Enterprise   6
     A1, Operate Department of Homeland Security   8
     A12, Provide & Maintain Resources   10
     A122, Provide & Maintain Human Resources   12
     A13, Accomplish the Priority Mission   14
     A2, Change Department of Homeland Security   16
     A23, Re-Design Department of Homeland Security   18
     A235, Re-Design Resources & Organization   20

III. HRMS Development   23
     Starting Point   23
     DHS Operations   24
     DHS Change   27

IV. Conclusion   33

Epilogue   35

Appendix — Graphic Modeling Language   37
     Basic Notation   38
     Diagram Hierarchy   39

Selected References   41

The Authors   42

Diagrams

Diagram A0. Operate & Change the Homeland Security Enterprise   7

Diagram A1. Operate Department of Homeland Security   9

Diagram A12. Provide & Maintain Resources   11

Diagram A122. Provide & Maintain Human Resources   13

Diagram A13. Accomplish the Priority Mission   15

Diagram A2. Change Department of Homeland Security   17

Diagram A23. Re-Design Department of Homeland Security   19

Diagram A235. Re-Design Resources & Organization   21

Figures

Figure 1. Syntax for Diagrams   4

Figure 2. Box & Arrow Syntax   38

Figure 3. Diagram Numbering   39

Tables

Table 1. Activity Hierarchy   5

Table 2. A0 in Diagram Hierarchy   7

Table 3. A1 in Diagram Hierarchy   9

Table 4. A12 in Diagram Hierarchy   11

Table 5. A122 in Diagram Hierarchy   13

Table 6. A13 in Diagram Hierarchy   15

Table 7. A2 in Diagram Hierarchy   17

Table 8. A23 in Diagram Hierarchy   19

Table 9. A235 in Diagram Hierarchy   21

Foreword

For the Federal Government, this is an age of unprecedented organizational complexity.

The creation of the Department of Homeland Security is among the largest restructurings in history. New legislation is transforming the nation's intelligence services, and many agencies are operating with new authorities to move out from under the restrictive human resources regulations of Title V.

Managing these changes successfully will require extraordinary effort and talent. It will require extensive and effective communications with a variety of stakeholders, including managers, supervisors, employees, labor unions, and Congressional staffers. And it will require a clear understanding of roles, responsibilities, and the decision making process.

In their monograph on Homeland Security Operations and Change, Al Small and Elizabeth Downey offer a systematic, structured approach to dealing with the massive DHS reorganization. While complex in itself on the surface, the Downey & Small approach – tested and proven in other federal agencies and in the private sector – provides a systematic framework for identifying the components of change and for clarifying the decisions that will be made as the Department creates new structures and systems. This framework has the potential for strengthening and speeding the change process, as well as improving communications among those responsible for the change.

I highly recommend a thorough review of the Downey & Small approach.

A. W. (Pete) Smith, Jr.
Senior Consultant, the Partnership for Public Service
Former President and CEO, Watson Wyatt Worldwide

Washington, D.C.
December, 2004

Preface

The Homeland Security Act of 2002, which established the U. S. Department of Homeland Security (DHS), recognizing the nature of the new DHS priority mission and the diverse personnel and policies of the 22 agencies it was bringing together as DHS, called for changes in human resource management. The Secretary of the Department of Homeland Security, jointly with the Director of the Office of Personnel Management (OPM), were authorized to establish a new Human Resources Management System (HRMS) for some or all of DHS. A Senior Review Advisory Committee (SRC) and a supporting Design Team were established with DHS, OPM and Union representatives to provide options.

The first SRC public meeting, held July 25, 2003 in Washington, D.C., was attended by the authors. The authors concluded that, although there was general agreement among the Committee and Team members on a number of principles, including the need for the HRMS to support the DHS mission, two important elements of change management were missing. The missing elements were *shared pictures* (1) of the interrelationships among the new HRMS activities, other resources provisioning activities, and the DHS mission operations, and (2) of the interrelationships among the change activities, including transitioning to a new HRMS, needed to more effectively and efficiently meet the DHS priority mission.

The HRMS design and implementation tasks, and their relationships with their context activities—particularly the new DHS priority mission operations—are complex. Without the shared picture, misunderstanding is likely and participants may fail to address some key interrelationships. Therefore, the authors developed a graphic model of relevant activities and relationships to offer as a management framework for DHS, OPM and other interested parties.

Excerpts from the model First Edition, with suggestions for consideration in establishing the HRMS, were presented to the SRC at its second public meeting, held October 20-22, 2003 in Washington, D.C. Excerpts from the model Second Edition were provided to DHS HR on March 18, 2004, with suggested revisions to the DHS HRMS Proposed Rule, February 20, 2004.

The Second Edition model (graphics and text) was published December 2004 to provide a management framework for communication, analysis and decision making in developing the new DHS HRMS as an integral component of DHS in support of the DHS mission.

Recent actions and public comments by the Department of Homeland Security have demonstrated weakness of policy and enforcement, and have pointed to a continuing need for clarity of missions and operating concepts. Strident statements and actions by some government employee unions have demonstrated a critical need for re-dedication to mission first.

The graphic Model DHS-HRMS-Version 2.0 remains useful, and so is being republished in this reformatted Third Edition with additional references.

I. Introduction

Background

The Department of Homeland Security (DHS) has begun the massive task of transitioning to an integrated, mission-focused enterprise. DHS was established by the Homeland Security Act of 2002 (HSA-2002), as a direct result of the devastating terrorist attacks of September 11, 2001. The first three elements of the DHS mission in HSA-2002: "(A) prevent terrorist attacks within the United States; (B) reduce the vulnerability of the United States to terrorism; and (C) minimize the damage, and assist in the recovery, from terrorist attacks that do occur within the United States." We call these three elements the DHS *priority mission.* [1, 2]

DHS was created with approximately 180 thousand employees from 22 agencies with different cultures, different personnel policies including classification and pay/promotion/benefit systems, and different labor relations, that must be brought together into an effective operation.

Human Resources Management

HSA-2002 gives the Secretary of Homeland Security tools for change. The Secretary may set up new, and change or discontinue (with limitations) existing, organizational units. Also, the Secretary, jointly with the Director of the Office of Personnel Management (OPM), may establish and adjust a new Human Resources Management System (HRMS) for some or all of DHS. Any new HRMS is required to be flexible, contemporary, and grounded in principles of merit and fitness.

A Senior Review Advisory Committee (SRC), made up of DHS and OPM senior executives, union leaders and experts, and a Design Team with broad representation, was established.[3]

The SRC was directed to provide the Secretary of DHS and Director of OPM with HRMS design options intended to produce an HRMS incorporating five key elements: (1) hire the brightest and best; (2) pay to be determined by individual merit and value to the organization; (3) classification to be fair and quantify value of work product to DHS; (4) a cooperative, positive work environment that benefits from employee input; and (5) accountability; i.e., individual performance to be linked to organizational goals. The HRMS elements and Congressional requirements describe a competent, competitive, flexible, mission-oriented workforce with performance-based pay and proper treatment.[4]

SRC members indicated that in the HRMS design, and in the creation of such a workforce, significant changes are needed from current government personnel systems. Most SRC members agreed that a change from an entitlement culture based on longevity,

---

[1] The Homeland Security Act of 2002, signed into law on 25 November 2002 as Public Law 107-296, established the Department of Homeland Security. The DHS mission, as defined in Section 101(b) of the Act, contains seven elements and is called the *primary mission* of DHS.

[2] The *National Strategy for Homeland Security*, 16 July 2002, establishes the strategic objectives for homeland security in order of priority: (1) Prevent terrorist attacks within the United States; (2) Reduce America's vulnerability to terrorism; and (3) Minimize the damage and recover from attacks that occur.

[3] The SRC was established for two years by the Secretary and first met 25 July 2003 (Federal Register, 11 July 2003).

[4] DHS Personnel System Fact Sheet, 1 April 2003

to a mission centered culture based on performance, is needed throughout DHS; Commissioner Bonner stated the HRMS must facilitate the mission, not impede it, and they could not simply fine-tune the General Schedule; Admiral Loy called for radical change; and, Director Basham said neither the status quo nor a tweak are an option—a new and different system is needed.[5, 6]

DHS leaders want to successfully compete with the private sector to hire the needed talent, to let go quickly those whose performance does not meet mission requirements, and to assign and re-assign people as operations dictate. They want to provide appropriate training and development, and to financially reward and retain top performers possessing valuable skills and experience. The leaders considered the current personnel systems cumbersome and unresponsive.

SRC members Ms Hausser and Mr. Sanders pointed out the foundational merit principle is sound, but its application has deteriorated so that poor performers are treated the same as the best. Development of a true performance measurement and reward system requires clear performance standards, as well as management wisdom, discipline and courage to act on those standards, consistent with appropriate employee protection. SRC Co-Chair, Ms. Hale, emphasized the need for staff involvement in both development and implementation. Mr. Smith said the main concern is two-way communications with employees from across the board.[7]

The importance and complexity of the HRMS change effort calls for careful implementation, including pilot testing, personnel feedback, and incremental phasing. Effective change demands strong, unwavering leadership, and a clear, commonly understood destination and roadmap, to maintain purposeful direction and momentum.

Operations & Change—Context for Human Resources Management

But where does design of a new HRMS start? The answer is suggested by an exchange among SRC members at the public meeting on 20 October 2003. Commissioner Bonner stated the first premise, which is the reason for DHS, to protect against terrorist threat; for this he needs specific skills and talents; he wants both performance and competency, and to provide increased pay based upon contribution to mission. Mr. Gage supported the needs but indicated most performance management systems have not worked in practice, since they assume incorrectly that competencies can be defined and written, and that supervisors are competent to rate performance among employees. Commissioner Bonner responded, and Mr. Sanders agreed, that a thoughtful system with management discipline would work. Mr. Aguirre added that metrics can be established, and private sector performance systems do work.

---

[5] SRC meeting, Washington, 20-22 Oct 2003 (Federal Register, 1 Oct 2003),

[6] Comments at the Oct 2003 SRC meeting by Robert Bonner, Commissioner of Customs and Border Protection; Admiral James M. Loy, Administrator, Transportation Security Administration (later Deputy Secretary, DHS); and, Ralph Basham, Director, United States Secret Service.

[7] Comments at Oct 2003 SRC meeting by Doris L. Hausser, Senior Policy Advisor, OPM; Ronald P. Sanders, Associate Director, Division for Strategic Human Resources Policy, OPM; Janet Hale, Undersecretary for Management, DHS; and, Pete Smith, President and CEO, The Private Sector Council.

Mr. Cohen said we should not let difficulty stop us. Finally, Ms Perez noted we start by understanding the mission, then ask what is needed to do that mission.[8]

We agree with Ms. Perez's starting point and expand her second question into the sequence "what are the needed principles, objectives and strategies, products and services, operating concepts, and total resources?" The answer to the question of operations concepts appears most difficult to articulate. Mission and operations concepts must be understood to define resources.

The new operations concepts, which describe how the DHS priority mission is to be accomplished, must be carefully designed for and clearly understood by each DHS area. These operations concept designs must be integrated both across DHS and with operations concepts of cooperating Federal agencies, state and local governments, and other organizations.

The operations concept designs are used to determine the requirements for resources, and for designing resource provisioning systems, in all areas; e.g., facilities, equipment, and human resources.

With new designs in hand, the transition approach can be developed for DHS mission operations, and resources provisioning and maintenance systems. Implementation of the new HRMS must be planned, resources prepared, and changes made—in coordination with the implementation of other new resources provisioning and maintenance systems, and in support of the new mission operations concepts for DHS.

Although human resources are the single most important DHS resource, the HRMS is only part of an overall human resources provisioning system, which is one component of the overall resources provisioning system required to support the DHS operations concepts and strategy for accomplishing the mission. Design and implementation of a new HRMS must be integral to the overall DHS design and transition.

Need for Graphic Model

Graphic modeling of mission operations, and resource provisioning and maintenance operations, can facilitate a clear shared view. A common understanding of the context of and requirements for the HRMS, must be maintained by the people involved throughout the long transition. The shared mental model is essential for communications, effective decision making, and long term commitment needed to fight complacency and bring about the necessary changes.[9]

The graphic model in this monograph contains a generic integrated picture of DHS operations and transition, which provides a contextual framework for HRMS design and implementation.

---

[8] Comments at Oct 2003 SRC Meeting by John Gage, President, American Federation of Government Employees; Eduardo Aguirre, Director, Bureau of Citizenship and Immigration Services; Steven R. Cohen, Senior Advisor for Homeland Security, OPM; and, Marta B. Perez, Associate Director, Division for Human Capital Leadership and Merit System Accountability, OPM.

---

[9] At the Oct 2003 SRC meeting, Admiral Loy expressed concern over increasing complacency as time passes since September 11, 2001.

Graphic Language

The graphic language used in this monograph's model is IDEF$_0$ (NIST 1993), which is derived from Structured Analysis and Design Technique (Ross 1977).

This graphic language, described in the Appendix, is used to portray activities and their relationships. An IDEF$_0$ model has a main activity, A0 composed of subactivities A1, A2, ... Each subactivity has its own subactivities; e.g., A1 contains A11, A12, ... The hierarchy of activities is broken out to the level of detail needed.

For each activity whose subactivities are defined in the model, there is an IDEF$_0$ diagram showing interdependencies among its subactivities.

The syntax used in the diagrams is straight forward as shown in Fig. 1.

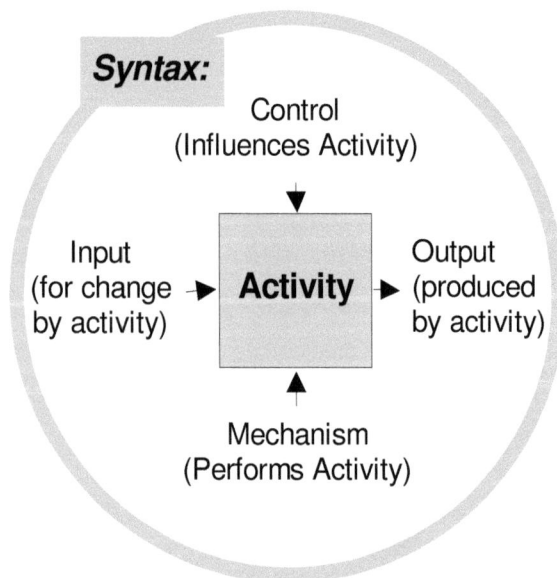

Each diagram in a model is usually presented full-size below a small copy of its "parent" diagram to quickly show context; i.e., Diagram Axy which shows the details of Activity Axy is presented below a small copy of Diagram Ax which shows the context of Activity Axy.

Presentation

The model is presented in hierarchical order in Section II. This provides an overall understanding of key activities and interrelationships, before discussing individual scenarios.

In Section III the model is used to present an approach for HRMS development focused on particular activities, interfaces, and sequencing as needed.

This two-stage presentation facilitates a common mental picture of the overall relationships as a basis for discussion of a particular development approach. If issues with the development approach emerge that cannot be resolved, then the overall model should be revisited to re-confirm its logic and correct any error discovered.

Syntax:

Control
(Influences Activity)

Input
(for change by activity) → **Activity** → Output
(produced by activity)

Mechanism
(Performs Activity)

Figure 1. Syntax for Diagrams

II. The Operations & Change Model

The purpose of this model is to provide a structured operations framework for use in managing design, planning, and implementation of a new HRMS. This model has a management viewpoint.

This model encompasses the Department of Homeland Security activities and their interdependencies in two major areas—operations and change. The model's top level activity, A0, Operate & Change the Homeland Security Enterprise, shown at the top of the activity hierarchy in Table 1, includes the activities of the entire homeland security enterprise. At the next level of detail the model focuses on DHS, broken out into two activities, A1, Operate DHS, and A2, Change DHS. Although change actually occurs within the operating enterprise, change is shown separately here to clarify the interrelationships among change activities.

Within the operations activity (A1) the model contains A13, Accomplish the Priority Mission and A12, Provide & Maintain Resources which are needed for the mission. Note that in addition to performing the mission, A13 contains associated operational resource management activities (A132, 134, 135) under direct control of the line management. The DHS management of human capital and the HRMS activities are principally in A122, Provide & Maintain Human Resources, a subactivity of A12.

The change activity (A2) contains

Re-Design DHS (A23) which includes Re-Design Resources & Organization (A235). The subactivity Re-Design Human Resources & System (A2352) designs the HR provision and maintenance system, which then operates in A122. Planning, preparing and implementing changes are done by A24, A25, and A26.

This model contains IDEF$_0$ diagrams corresponding to activities highlighted in the Activity Hierarchy of Table 1.

Table 1. Activity Hierarchy

[A0] Operate & Change the Homeland Security Enterprise
  [A1] Operate Department of Homeland Security
    [A11] Direct DHS
    [A12] Provide & Maintain Resources
      [A121] Direct Overall Resource Provisioning
      [A122] Provide & Maintain Human Resources
        [A1221] Direct HR Provisioning and Maintenance
        [A1222] Acquire, Classify, Assign, Retire, etc.
        [A1223] Support & Develop Human Resources
        [A1224] Operate Performance Eval. & Pay Systems
        [A1225] Conduct Adverse Actions/ Appeals
        [A1226] Conduct Labor Relations
      [A123] Provide & Maintain Other Resources
    [A13] Accomplish the Priority Mission
      [A131] Plan and Control Mission Operations
      [A132] Check-In, Bring-up-to- Speed, Put On-Line
      [A133] Conduct Priority Mission Operations
      [A134] Eval.Mission Accomplish., Resource Perform.& Sit.
      [A135] Locally Sustain/Repair, Hold/Release, Check-Out
  [A2] Change Department of Homeland Security
    [A21] Manage DHS Change
    [A22] Conduct Analyses & Predictions
    [A23] Re-Design Department of Homeland Security
      [A231] Re-Envision DHS & ID Principles
      [A232] Re-Devise Objectives & Strategies
      [A233] Re-Design Products & Services
      [A234] Re-Design DHS Operations
      [A235] Re-Design Resources & Organization
        [A2351] Re-Specify Resources & Organization Requirem'ts
        [A2352] Re-Design Human Resources & System
        [A2353] Re-Design Other Resources & Systems
        [A2354] Re-Design Organization, Assignments, & Mgt Syste
        [A2355] Integrate & Evaluate Total Design
    [A24] Plan to Implement Changes
    [A25] Prepare Resources to Implement
    [A26] Implement Changes

DHS-HRMS v.2.0, © 2004, D&S

A0, Operate & Change the Homeland Security Enterprise

United States Homeland Security is provided by a group of organizations composed of the new Department of Homeland Security (DHS) and other entities (e.g., CIA, FBI, DoD, state and local governments, private organizations, and allied governments). This group, under the oversight of DHS, must function as a virtual enterprise to protect U.S. homeland resources from terrorist attack and neutralize hostile resources conducting or supporting terrorist activities against the U.S. homeland.

The enterprise operations of DHS and other agencies, shown as A1, et.al. in Diagram A0 facing, act together upon the U.S., Friendly, and Hostile Resources to produce a Protected U.S. Homeland and Neutralized Hostile Resources. Neither DHS nor any other single agency accomplishes this mission alone, but must coordinate operations and handoff "work-in-progress." Some examples of operational handoff include: (a) terrorists captured by U.S. military forces may be turned over to CIA for questioning; (b) a suspicious vessel on the high seas detected by the Navy may be handed-off to the Coast Guard as the vessel nears the U.S. coastline, and later handed off to DHS Border Protection.

DHS operations (A1) monitor the U.S., friendly and hostile situation directly, and indirectly via other agencies, in order to identify threats and determine appropriate responses. DHS issues alerts and keeps the NCA and others informed of the Homeland Security situation.

Transition from separate operating agencies into the new DHS requires coordination with changes in supporting enterprises (A2, et.al.) to ensure effective integrated operations (A1). Further, the continuous and changing terrorist threat requires continuous situation-monitoring and change. DHS change activities must respond in a timely manner to unanticipated threats uncovered while conducting current operations (in A1) or change-analysis (within A2). If the threat is immediate, emergency change may be required; if near-term, an urgent change; otherwise it should be handled by the comprehensive integrated change program.[10]

People conducting operations (A1) must be kept involved in current and planned change activities (A2) to contribute their knowledge and perspective, and reduce their resistance to change.

Table 2 on the facing page shows A0 in the diagram hierarchy. Diagram A0, at bottom of the facing page, shows key relationships among the subactivities of A0. The small A-0, parent diagram of A0, at top right of the facing page is the context diagram of the overall model.

---

[10] A comprehensive integrated approach ensures time-critical projects are not impeded by long-range, integrated program constraints, and immediate pressures do not dissolve the long range program into disjoint efforts (Small and Downey 2001).

Table 2. A0 in Diagram Hierarchy	
Diag.	**Activity**
A0	Operate & Change the Homeland Security Enterprise
A1	Operate Department of Homeland Security
A12	Provide & Maintain Resources
A122	Provide & Maintain Human Resources
A13	Accomplish the Priority Mission
A2	Change Department of Homeland Security
A23	Re-Design Department of Homeland Security
A235	Re-Design Resources & Organization

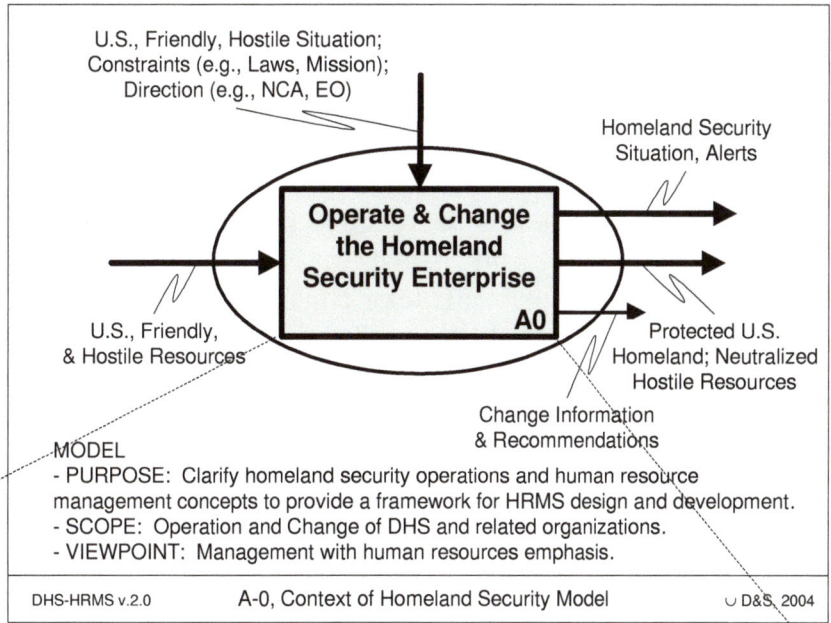

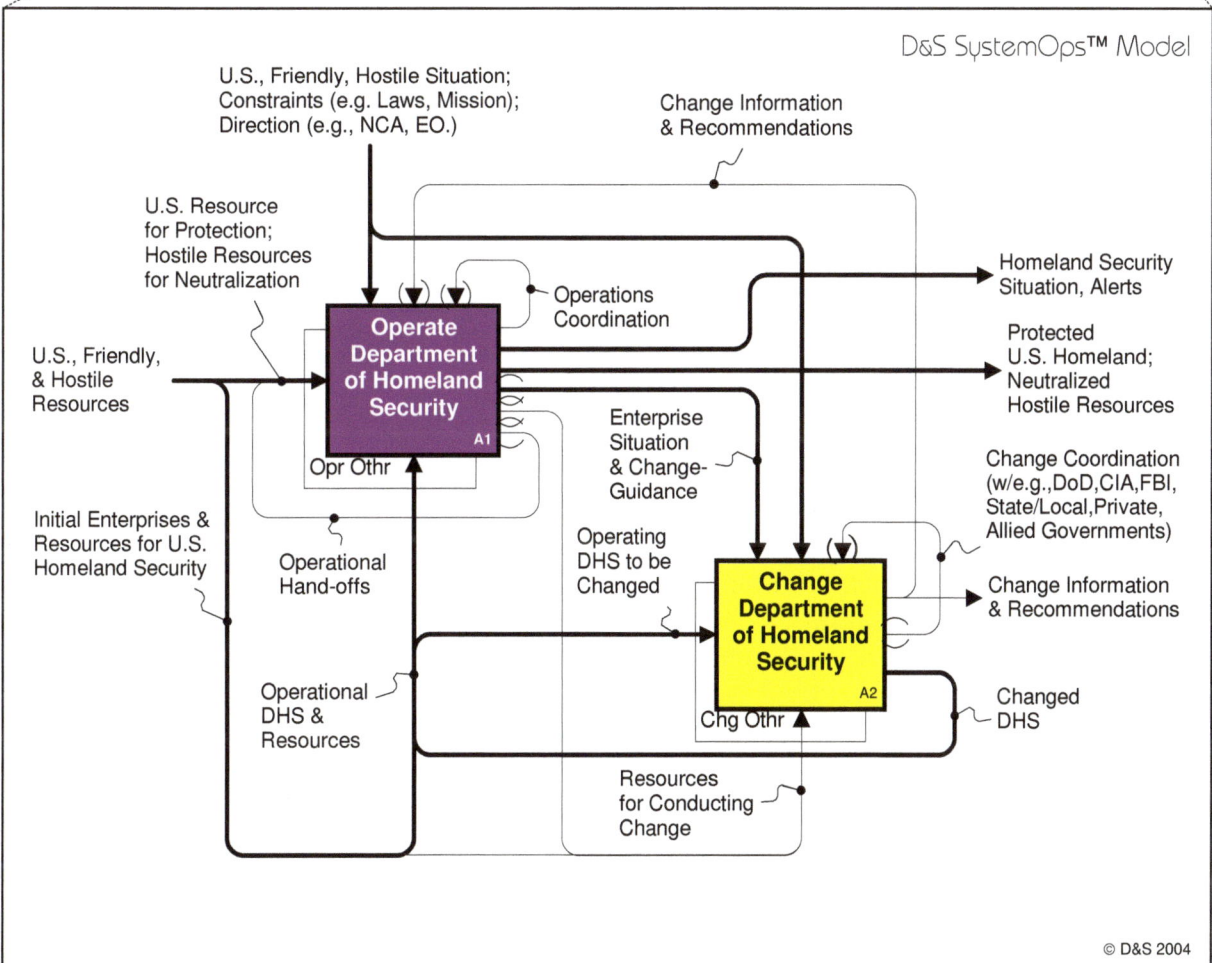

U.S., Friendly, Hostile Situation; Constraints (e.g., Laws, Mission); Direction (e.g., NCA, EO)

Operate & Change the Homeland Security Enterprise

A0

Homeland Security Situation, Alerts

U.S., Friendly, & Hostile Resources

Protected U.S. Homeland; Neutralized Hostile Resources

Change Information & Recommendations

MODEL
- PURPOSE: Clarify homeland security operations and human resource management concepts to provide a framework for HRMS design and development.
- SCOPE: Operation and Change of DHS and related organizations.
- VIEWPOINT: Management with human resources emphasis.

DHS-HRMS v.2.0   A-0, Context of Homeland Security Model   ∪ D&S, 2004

D&S SystemOps™ Model

U.S., Friendly, Hostile Situation; Constraints (e.g. Laws, Mission); Direction (e.g., NCA, EO.)

Change Information & Recommendations

U.S. Resource for Protection; Hostile Resources for Neutralization

Operations Coordination

Operate Department of Homeland Security
A1
Opr Othr

U.S., Friendly, & Hostile Resources

Homeland Security Situation, Alerts

Protected U.S. Homeland; Neutralized Hostile Resources

Enterprise Situation & Change-Guidance

Initial Enterprises & Resources for U.S. Homeland Security

Operational Hand-offs

Operating DHS to be Changed

Change Department of Homeland Security
A2
Chg Othr

Change Coordination (w/e.g.,DoD,CIA,FBI, State/Local,Private, Allied Governments)

Change Information & Recommendations

Operational DHS & Resources

Changed DHS

Resources for Conducting Change

© D&S 2004

Diagram A0, Operate & Change Homeland Security Enterprise   DHS-HRMS v.2.0

A1, Operate Department of Homeland Security

The priority mission of the new DHS is to prevent terrorist attacks within the United States, reduce the vulnerability of the United States to terrorism, and minimize damage, and assist in the recovery, from terrorist attacks that do occur within the United States.

This model emphasizes accomplishing the priority mission, which is the reason for creating the new DHS. While other functions are to be continued they must not interfere with the priority mission.

DHS operations (shown in the A1 diagram facing) are described in terms of three sub-activities: (1) Direct DHS; (2) Provide & Maintain Resources; (3) Accomplish the Priority (and Other) Mission.

A11, Direct DHS.

Directing the new DHS includes directing the cabinet level department headquarters and the included agencies such as USCG, USSS, TSA, USC&BP, and FEMA. DHS issues alerts and communicates the Homeland Security situation to the NCA and appropriate organizations.

A12, Provide & Maintain Resources.

Provision and maintenance of resources includes providing human resources, equipment, facilities, and budget in response to resource requirements (from A13) for accomplishing the mission (in A13). The resource provision activity also provides the resources needed for directing DHS (A11) and for its own functions (A12).

This activity keeps the direction and mission activities informed of the resource situation, and complies with direction and constraints from DHS and higher authority.

A13, Accomplish the Priority Mission.

Accomplishment of the priority mission requires DHS monitor the U.S., friendly and hostile situation to determine and then take appropriate action to protect the U.S. Homeland and neutralize hostile resources.

The mission activity must articulate its resources requirements and evaluate their performance. Included are staff promotion decisions in accordance with DHS and higher authority policy direction. This activity also makes mission decisions including application of resources; it may transfer resources between operations (A13), and it may return resources for provisioning and maintenance activities (A12) as it deems necessary.

Table 3 facing shows A1 in the diagram hierarchy. Diagram A1 is shown on facing page bottom with a miniature of its parent diagram A0 above it.

Diag.	Activity
	Table 3. A1 in Diagram Hierarchy
A0	Operate & Change the Homeland Security Enterprise
A1	Operate Department of Homeland Security
A12	Provide & Maintain Resources
A122	Provide & Maintain Human Resources
A13	Accomplish the Priority Mission
A2	Change Department of Homeland Security
A23	Re-Design Department of Homeland Security
A235	Re-Design Resources & Organization

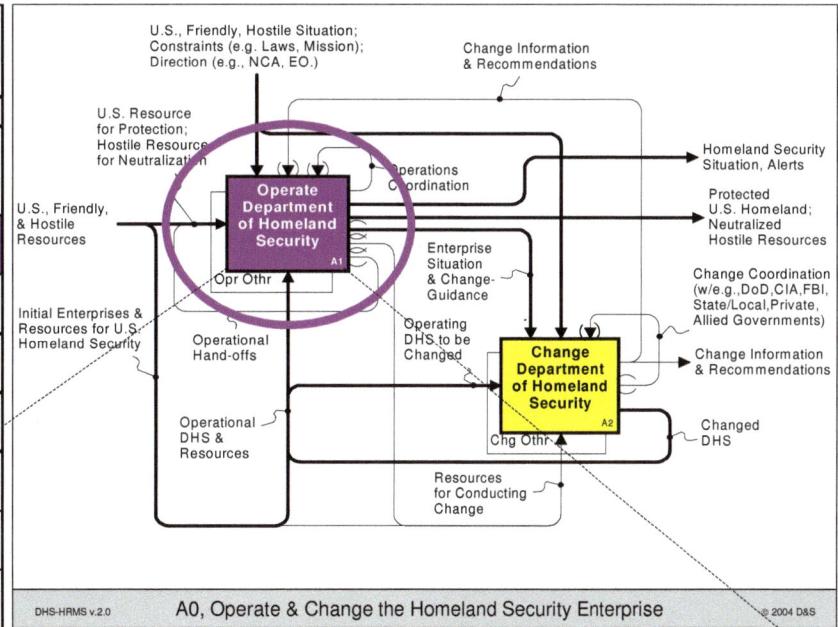

DHS-HRMS v.2.0 — A0, Operate & Change the Homeland Security Enterprise — © 2004 D&S

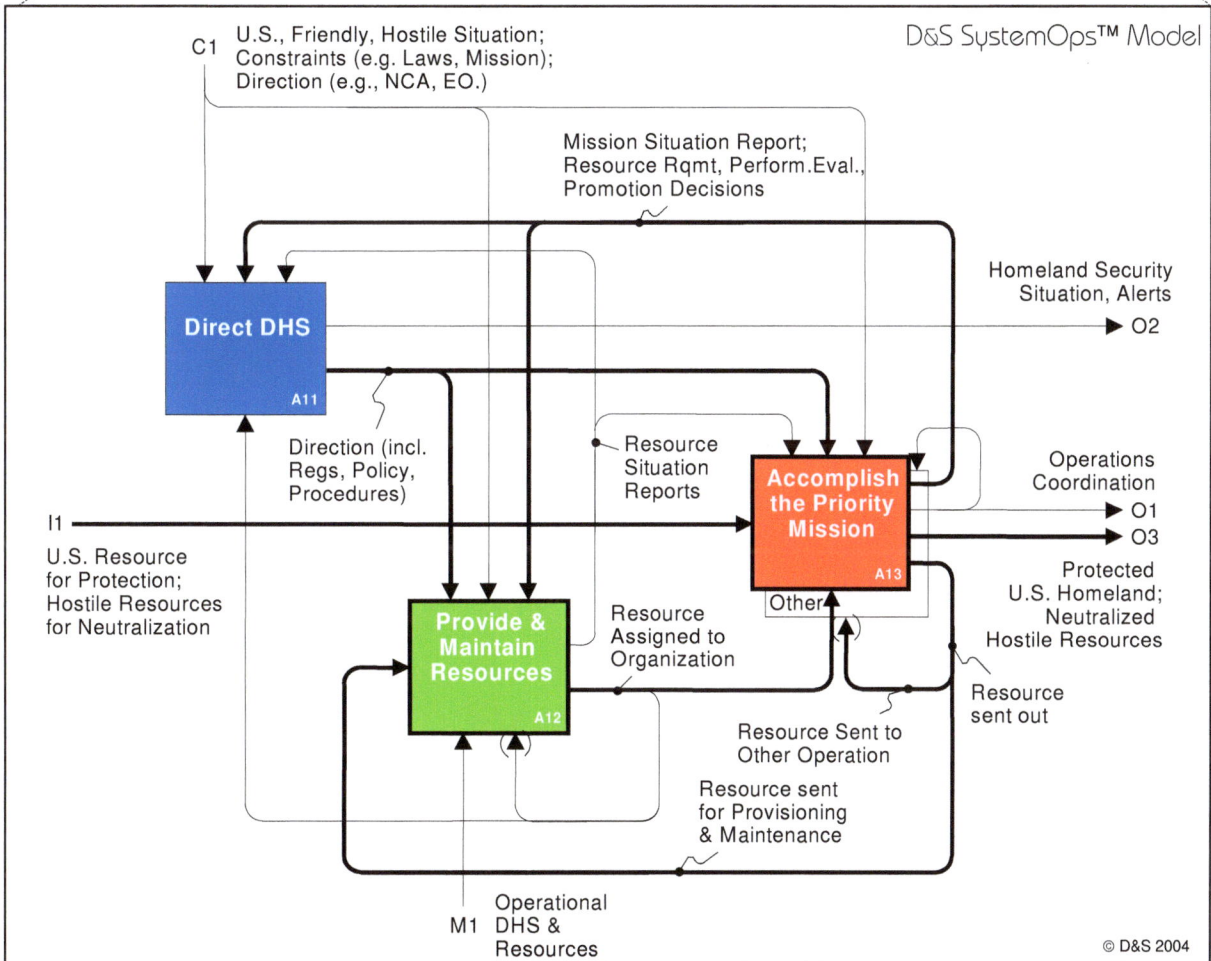

D&S SystemOps™ Model

© D&S 2004

Diagram A1, Operate Department of Homeland Security   DHS-HRMS v.2.0

A12, Provide & Maintain Resources

Provision and maintenance of resources includes providing of human resources, equipment, and facilities, in response to resource requirements to accomplish the priority mission.[11]

The resource provision activity also provides the resources needed for its own operations and for direction of DHS. This activity keeps the direction and mission activities informed of the resource situation, and complies with direction and constraints from DHS and higher authority.

Diagram A12 facing shows this activity composed of three sub-activities: (1) Direct Overall Resource Provisioning; (2) Provide & Maintain Human Resources; (3) Provide & Maintain Other Resources.

A121, Direct Overall Resource Provisioning.

Direction of overall resource provisioning is required to ensure integrated resources. Overall direction also provides an activity with authority to re-direct any/all resources provisioning in an integrated fashion needed to support unanticipated mission emergencies, without multiple-management approval delays.[12,13]

A122, Provide & Maintain Human Resources.

The provision of human resources is highlighted in this model. This activity acquires, trains, assigns and maintains human resources in response to human resource requirements, performance reports, and promotion decisions from the mission activities in A13.

This activity keeps the overall management informed of human resources status and issues, and conducts direct informal coordination as needed for the provision of other resources.

Although the new DHS Human Resource Management System (HRMS) is operated and sustained in A122, it operates to facilitate management decisions in A11, A121, and A13 regarding human resources.

A123, Provide & Maintain Other Resources.

All other resources needed to perform the mission must also be responsive to requirements, keep overall management informed of their resources situations, and coordinate directly to accomplish the mission in a timely fashion.

---

[11] At the Oct 2003 SRC meeting, Prof. Maurice McTigue, Visiting Scholar at George Mason University, enumerated three principal modes of homeland security operations—status quo, high risk, and under attack. He pointed out the need to consider how to structure the HRMS to meet the expanded mission, and how to deploy differently in each mode—not in generalities, but explicitly; e.g., the specific skills which will be needed in each situation.

[12] The U.S. Marine Corps Combat Development Process was established to ensure integration of all activities needed to generate combat-ready Marine Air-Ground Task Forces. A graphic model was developed to sharpen the concept and communicate the leadership vision (USMC 1994)

---

[13] Within the DHS organization, direction of overall resource provisioning (A121) is performed by the Undersecretary for Management, Janet Hale.

Table 4. A12 in Diagram Hierarchy	
Diag.	Activity
A0	Operate & Change the Homeland Security Enterprise
A1	Operate Department of Homeland Security
A12	Provide & Maintain Resources
A122	Provide & Maintain Human Resources
A13	Accomplish the Priority Mission
A2	Change Department of Homeland Security
A23	Re-Design Department of Homeland Security
A235	Re-Design Resources & Organization

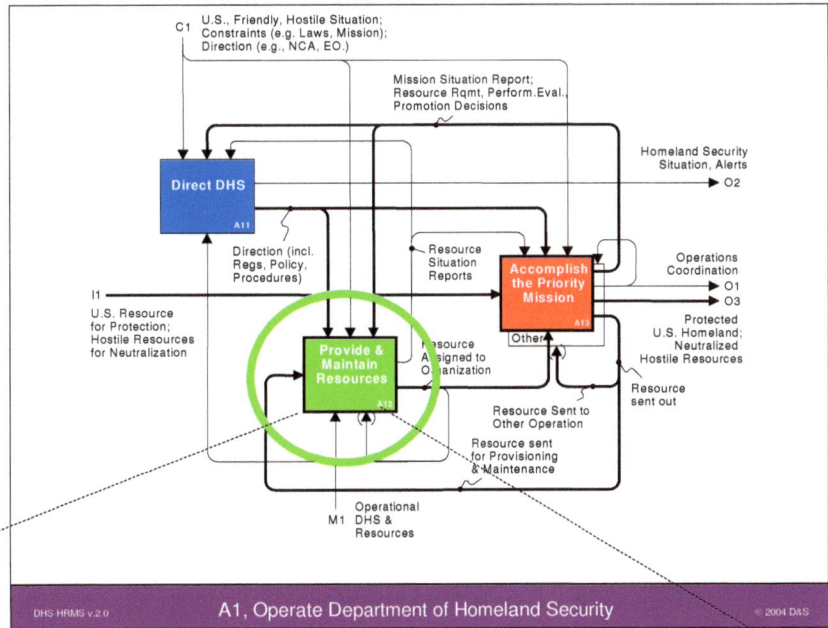

A1, Operate Department of Homeland Security

DHS-HRMS v.2.0   © 2004 D&S

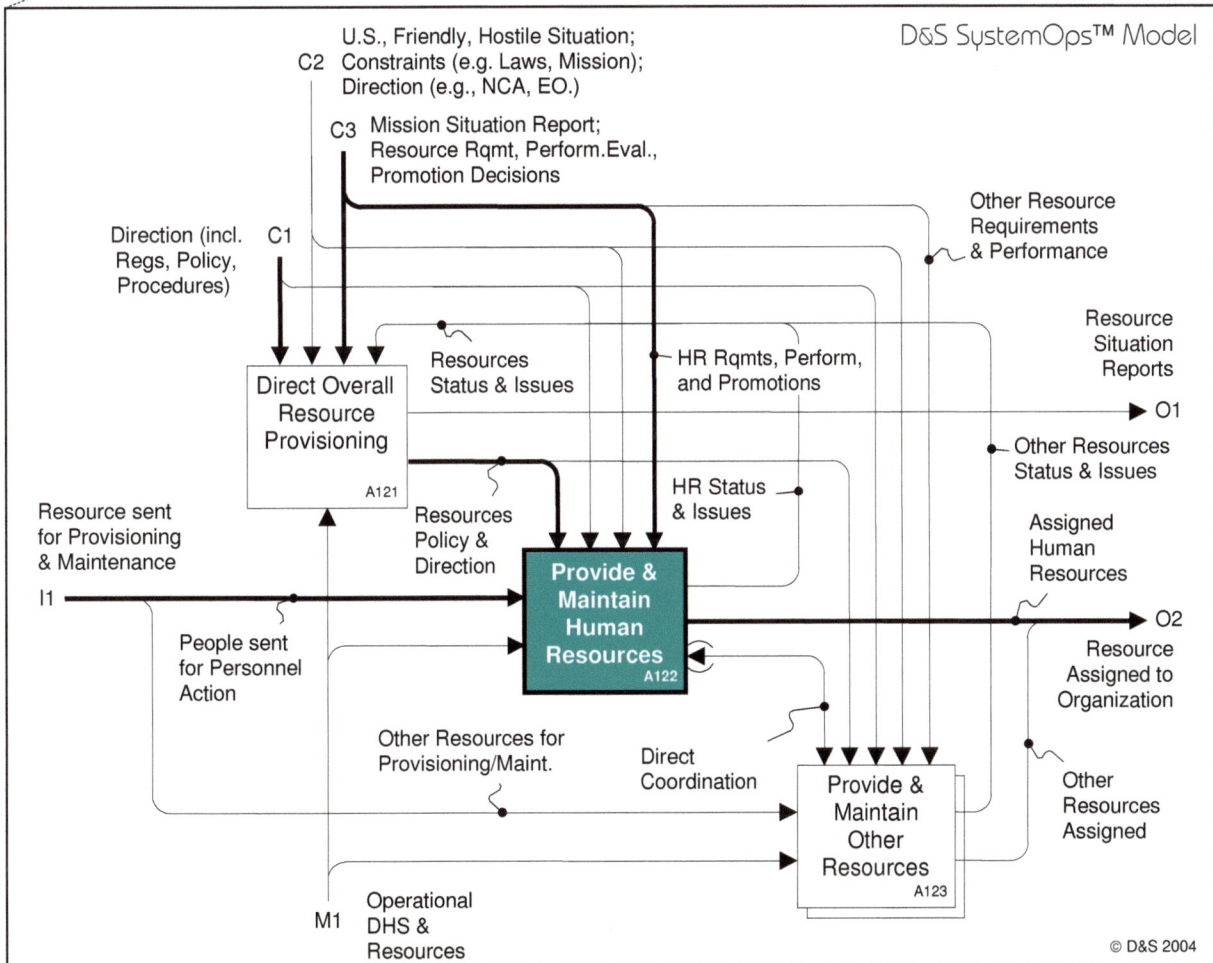

D&S SystemOps™ Model

© D&S 2004

Diagram A12, Provide & Maintain Resources

DHS-HRMS v.2.0

A122, Provide & Maintain Human Resources

The concept of operations for providing and maintaining human resources must be clearly defined in order to design an appropriate Human Resources Management System (HRMS).[14]

Diagram A122 facing provides a generic framework for the HR provisioning system in terms of six sub-activities: (1) Direct HR Provisioning & Maintenance; (2) Acquire, Classify, Assign, Retire, etc.; (3) Support & Develop Human Resources; (4) Operate Performance Evaluation & Pay System; (5) Conduct Adverse Actions/Appeals; and, (6) Conduct Labor Relations.

A1221, Direct HR Provisioning & Maintenance.

In response to human resources requirements, consistent with the mission situation and HR Situation Reports, this management activity directs the total human resources provisioning and maintenance for DHS, consistent with regulations, policy and direction from higher authority. *HR Status & Issues* are reported to the overall resource provisioning activity.

A1222, Acquire, Classify, Assign, Retire, etc.

This principal subactivity within HR, hires and fires, classifies, assigns and re-assigns, sends staff for training, and maintains the staff roster.

A1223, Support & Develop Human Resources.

This activity supports and develops staff members and includes training of staff. Developed personnel and their training reports are passed back to A1222, where staff member classification and the roster are updated, and newly trained personnel are assigned to use their new training.

A1224, Operate Performance Evaluation & Pay Systems.

Employees are paid by this activity in accordance with the staff *Roster* from the classification activity (in A1222) and HR Direction from HR management (in A1221). *HR Performance* reports and *Promotion* decisions from mission management (in A13) are reviewed and recorded. This activity should confirm adjustments to the Roster are consistent with the performance and promotion information received. When negative performance evaluations meet certain criteria set in HR, this activity notifies the adverse action activity (in A1225).

A1225, Conduct Adverse Actions/Appeals.

Adverse actions are initiated in response to negative performance reports per *HR Direction*. Employees and/or their reps may initiate appeals of adverse actions, or of selected personnel actions, e.g., classification, assignment, performance evaluation, and promotion.

A1226, Conduct Labor Relations.

DHS conducts labor relations consistent with *HR Direction*, with consideration of *Employee Representative Inputs*.

---

[14] At the Oct 2003 SRC meeting, Prof. Patricia Ingraham, Syracuse University, said we need to think about the HR system as an 'integrated whole' (e.g., classification cannot be separated from hiring); Mr. Aguirre, agreed.

Diag.	Activity
A0	Operate & Change the Homeland Security Enterprise
A1	Operate Department of Homeland Security
A12	Provide & Maintain Resources
A122	Provide & Maintain Human Resources
A13	Accomplish the Priority Mission
A2	Change Department of Homeland Security
A23	Re-Design Department of Homeland Security
A235	Re-Design Resources & Organization

Table 5. A122 in Diagram Hierarchy

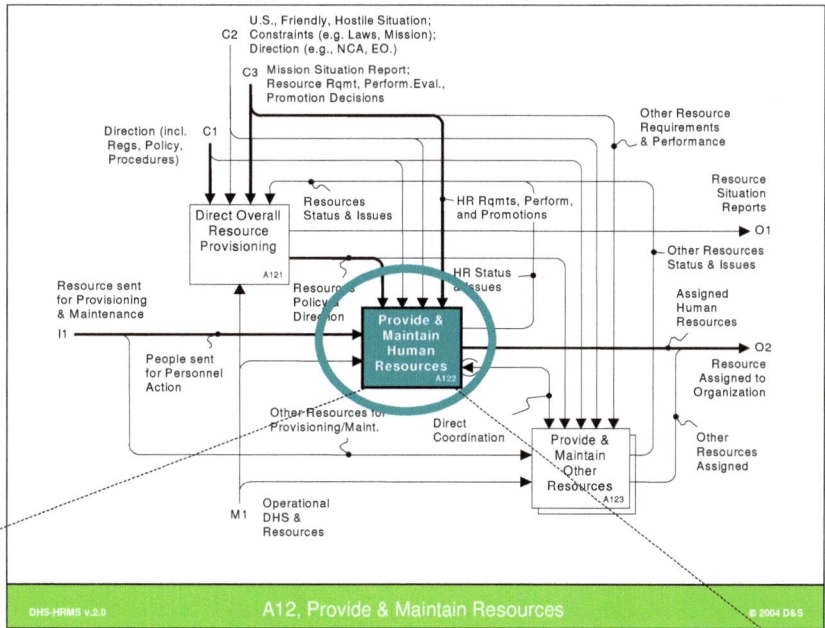

A12, Provide & Maintain Resources

DHS-HRMS v.2.0   © 2004 D&S

D&S SystemOps™ Model

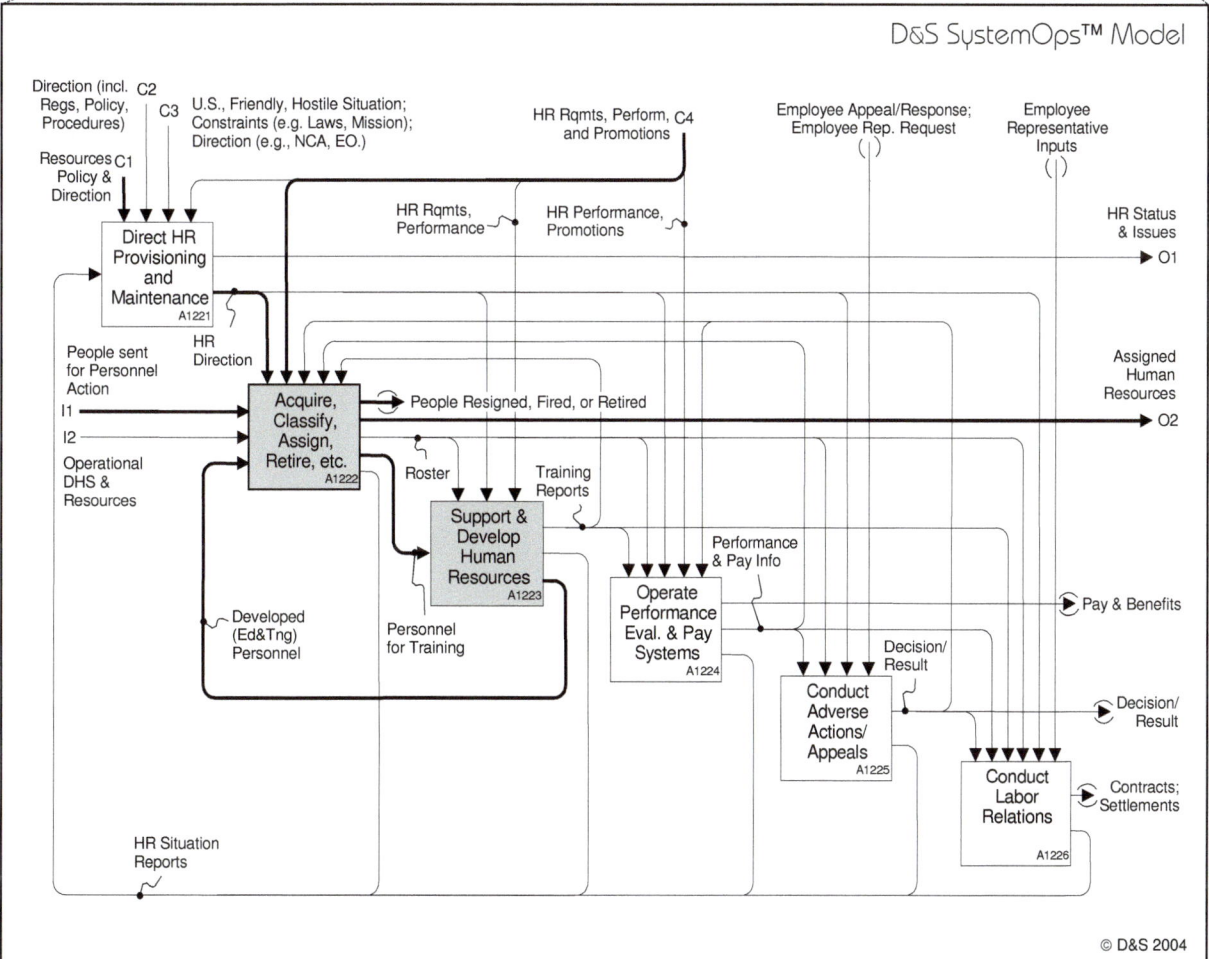

© D&S 2004

Diagram A122, Provide & Maintain Human Resources

DHS-HRMS v.2.0

A13, Accomplish the Priority Mission

The DHS priority responsibilities include information analysis and infrastructure protection; chemical, biological, radiological, nuclear, and related countermeasures; border and transport security; emergency prep and response; and coordination with other Federal agencies, State and local authorities, and the private sector.

This mission requires coordinated operations of numerous functions acting upon *U.S. Resource for Protection* and *Hostile Resources for Neutralization*, in response to the situation and direction, to produce a *Protected U.S. Homeland* and *Neutralized Hostile Resources*. Specifics of each category of mission function must be known before resource requirements are specified and provisioning systems designed.[15]

Diagram A13 facing shows a generic model of five sub-activities to Accomplish the Priority Mission: (1) Plan and Control Mission Op'ns; (2) Check-In, Bring-up-to-Speed, Put On-Line (Resources); (3) Conduct Priority Mission Op'ns; (4) Evaluate Mission Accomplishm't, Resources Performance, and Situation; and, (5) Locally Sustain or Repair, Hold or Release, Check-Out (Resources).

A131, Plan and Control Mission Op'ns.

In response to direction and the situation, actions are planned and *Orders & Instructions* are issued to the priority mission operations and resources handling activities. This activity is responsible for formal *Op'ns Coordination*, *Mission Situation Rpts*, *Resource Requirements*, *Performance Evaluation*, and *Promotion Decisions*.

A132, Check-In, Bring-up-to-Speed, Put On-Line.

The line manager assesses condition of resources and decides when they are ready to be put on-line for mission operations. He/she also decides if arriving resources are held aside for later use or returned to provisioning.

A133, Conduct Priority Mission Op'ns.

On-Line Resources are applied to conduct mission operations as directed. Operations are coordinated with other units, and *Observations* of mission accomplishment, resource performance, and situation are reported.

A134, Evaluate Mission Accomplishm't, Resources Perform. & Sit.

Mission accomplishment and resource performance are evaluated to make necessary adjustments in the planning and conduct of priority mission operations. The evaluation activity should also take note and report any need for change in the enterprise op'ns.

A135, Locally Sustain/Repair, Hold/Release, Check-Out.

Resources Coming Off Duty may be sustained or repaired, held or released, shifted to other mission op'ns, or sent to provisioning (A12).

---

[15] At the Oct 2003 SRC meeting, Ms Hausser acknowledged there can be different HR systems where it makes sense strategically. Mr. Smith said those differences should be decided by [line] management and not HR; however, there needs to be core common principles. Mr. Basham concurred that core common principles are very important.

Table 6. A13 in Diagram Hierarchy

Diag.	Activity
A0	Operate & Change the Homeland Security Enterprise
A1	Operate Department of Homeland Security
A12	Provide & Maintain Resources
A122	Provide & Maintain Human Resources
A13	**Accomplish the Priority Mission**
A2	Change Department of Homeland Security
A23	Re-Design Department of Homeland Security
A235	Re-Design Resources & Organization

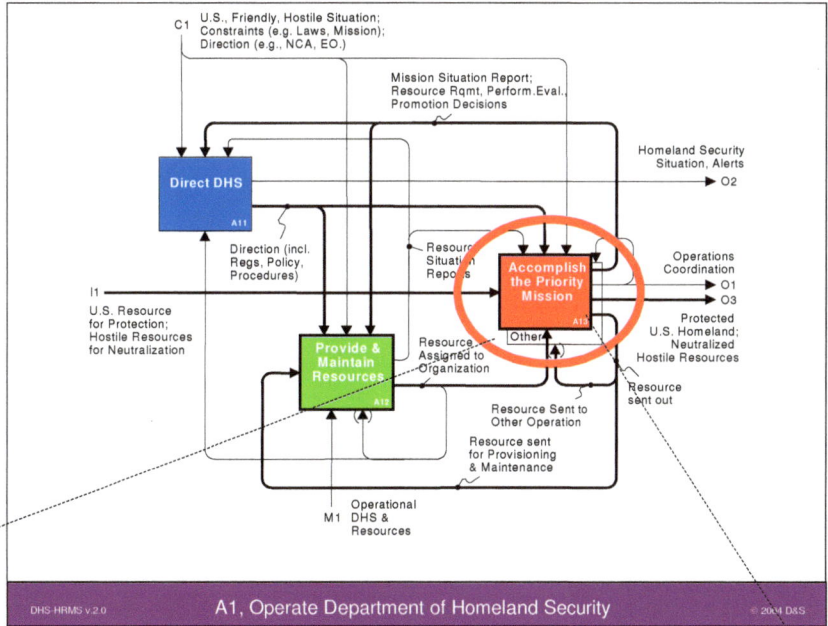

A1, Operate Department of Homeland Security

DHS-HRMS v.2.0   © 2004 D&S

D&S SystemOps™ Model

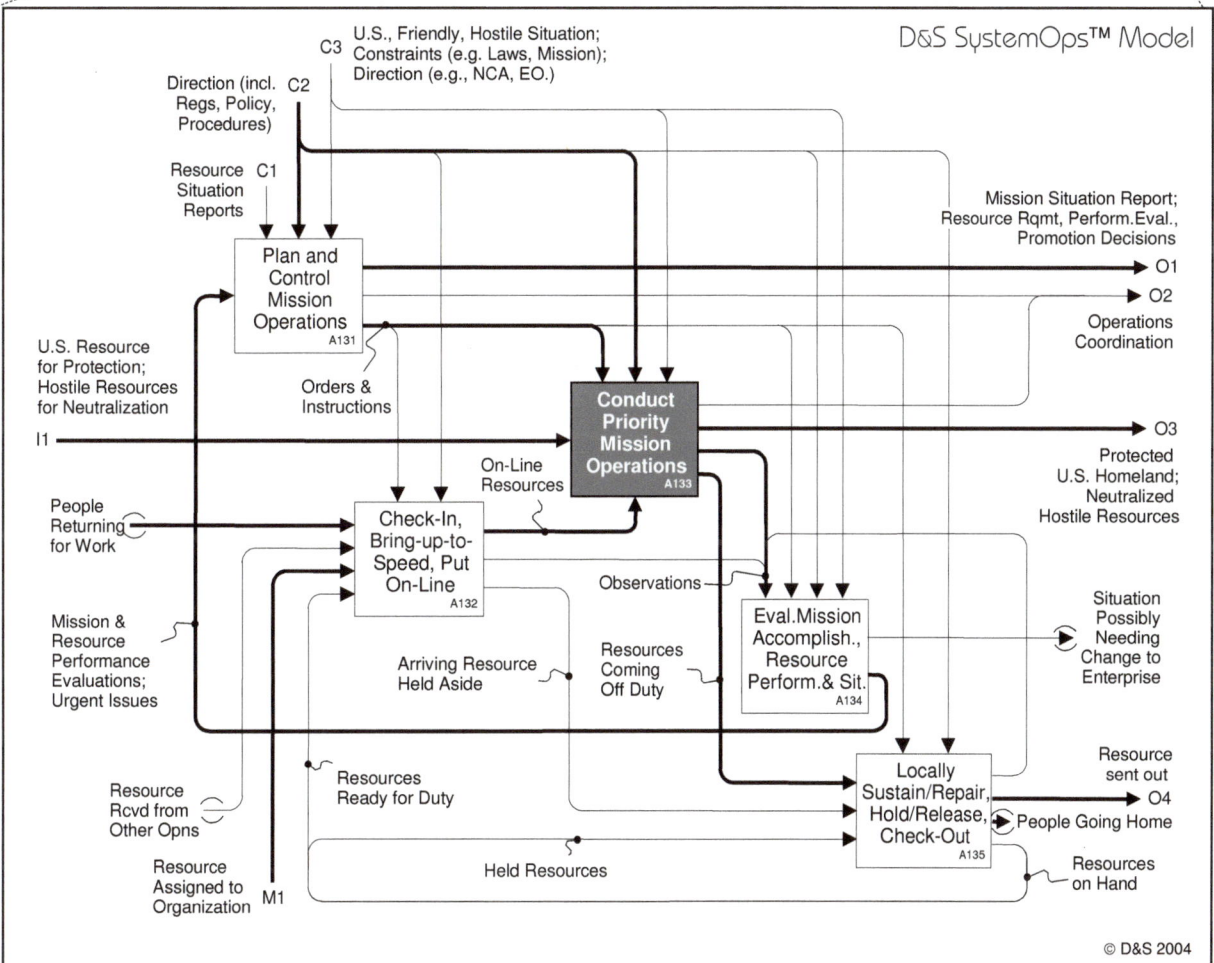

© D&S 2004

Diagram A13, Accomplish the Priority Mission

DHS-HRMS v.2.0

A2, Change Department of Homeland Security

Transition of the separate entities that make up the new DHS into a single department is the biggest enterprise change effort since formation of the Department of Defense. Although HSA-2002 sets a one-year transition period, the changing nature of the threat and improvements in technology, and the learning curve in the new arena of homeland security, will necessitate continuing enterprise changes.

Diagram A2 shows the change activity composed of six sub-activities: (1) Manage DHS Change; (2) Conduct Analyses & Predictions; (3) Re-Design Department of Homeland Security; (4) Plan to Implement Changes; (5) Prepare Resources to Implement; (6) Implement Changes.

A21, Manage DHS Change.
The management activity guides and directs the overall change process from conception and analysis through implementation, and directs a mix of urgent and comprehensive changes.[16]

A22, Conduct Analyses & Predictions.
The analysis & prediction activities, guided by change-direction, examine the enterprise and environment situations to produce current analyses and predictions for use in managing changes, re-designing the enterprise, and planning implementation of changes.[17]

A23, Re-Design Department of Homeland Security.
In response to *Change-Direction*, a new *DHS Design* is developed to address the *Current Analyses & Predictions* of *U.S., Friendly, Hostile Situation*, while considering *Implementation Issues with Design*. Legal constraints and directions from higher authority are incorporated in the *Change-Direction*. This activity sends its specific *Analysis Needs* to A22.

A24, Plan to Implement Changes.
Implementation planning should start early with the draft DHS designs to identify any *Implementation Issue*. The plan provides for preparation and testing of resources for change, prior to change implementation. Phased implementation of major changes should be considered.

A25, Prepare Resources to Implement.
Resources for conducting change are prepared and tested off-line prior to implementation to reduce disruption to operations during switch-over. This includes hiring and training of new personnel, as well as training of transferees in the pipeline before starting their new duties.

A26, Implement Changes.
Implementation of changes to the operating DHS requires transition during operations. This transition is scheduled to minimize disruption to critical services, and needs to be monitored to ensure serious failures are quickly addressed. The implementation activity must be able and ready to switch back to the original configuration and restore operations. A26 also conducts On-Job-Training.

---

[16] Urgent changes and comprehensive changes need differentiated treatment (Small and Downey 2001).

[17] A comprehensive framework for managing collection, analysis and prediction for deciding enterprise change has been developed (Small and Downey 2005).

Table 7. A2 in Diagram Hierarchy	
Diag.	**Activity**
A0	Operate & Change the Homeland Security Enterprise
A1	Operate Department of Homeland Security
A12	Provide & Maintain Resources
A122	Provide & Maintain Human Resources
A13	Accomplish the Priority Mission
A2	Change Department of Homeland Security
A23	Re-Design Department of Homeland Security
A235	Re-Design Resources & Organization

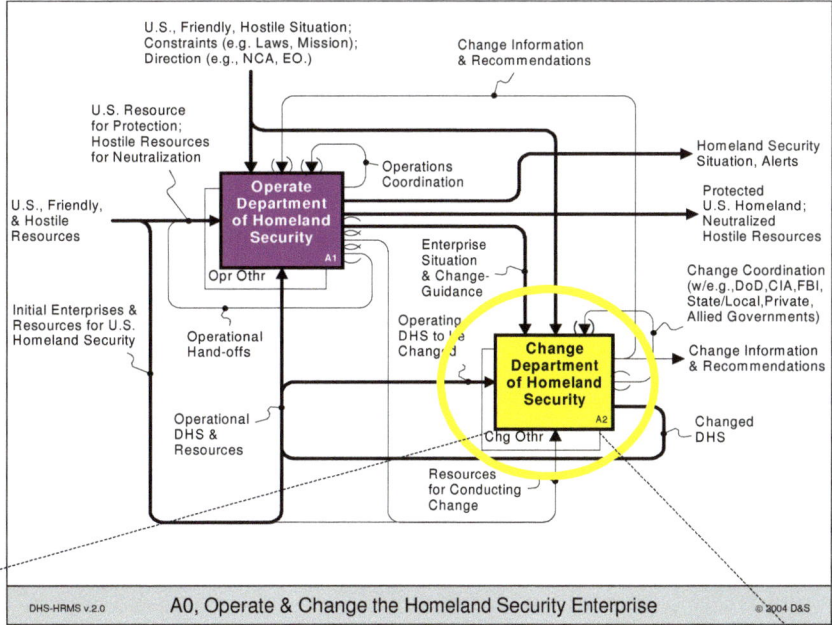

A0, Operate & Change the Homeland Security Enterprise

DHS-HRMS v.2.0   © 2004 D&S

D&S SystemOps™ Model

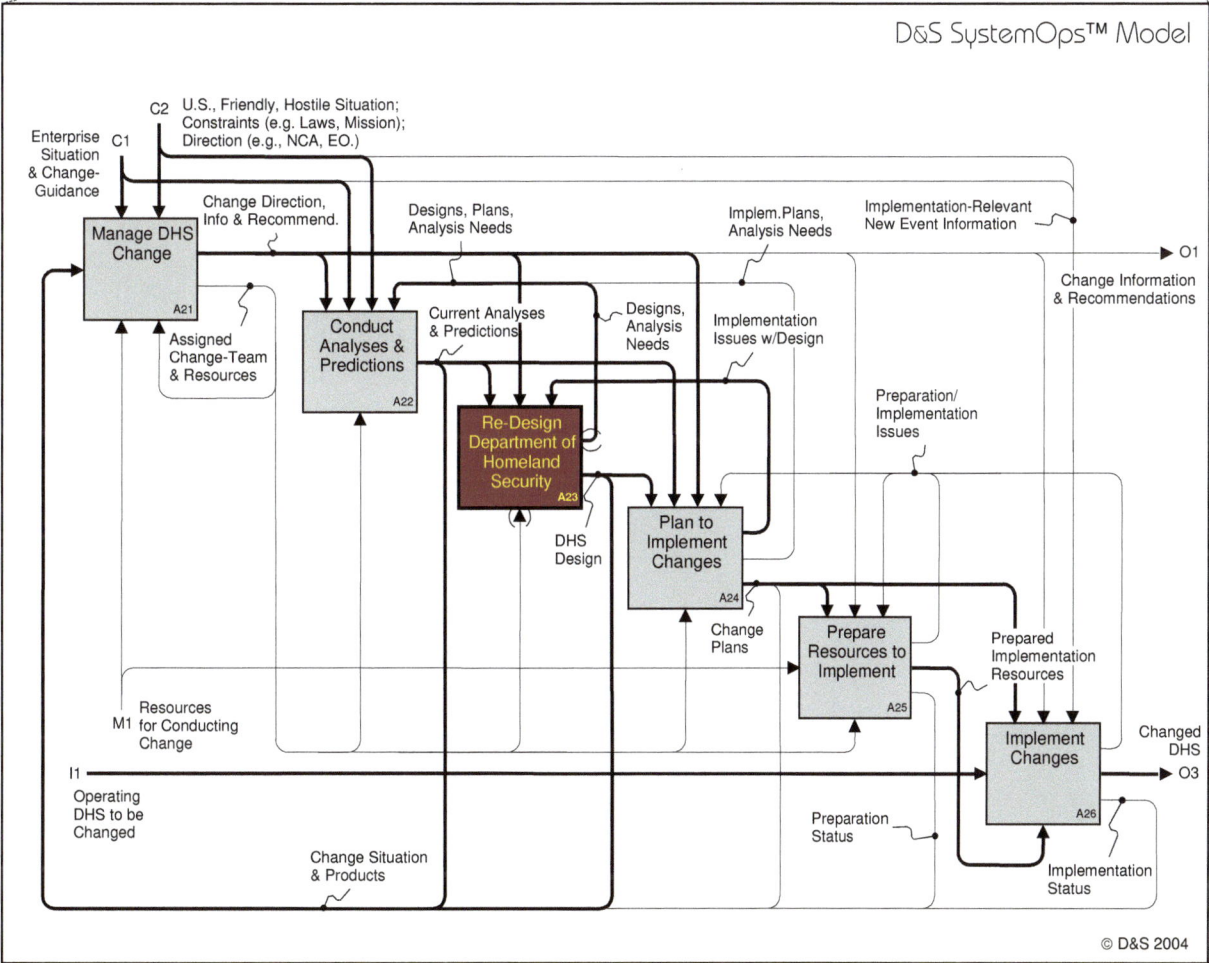

© D&S 2004

Diagram A2, Change Department of Homeland Security   DHS-HRMS v.2.0

A23, Re-Design Department of Homeland Security

In response to *Change-Direction*, a new *DHS Design* is developed to address the *Current Analyses & Predictions* from A22 concerning *U.S., Friendly, Hostile Situation*. Legal constraints and directions from higher authority are incorporated in the *Change-Direction* from A21. The A23 design activity requests needed analyses from A22 and keeps A22 informed of new designs.

In Diagram A23, Re-Design Department of Homeland Security contains five sub-activities: (1) Re-Envision DHS & ID Principles; (2) Re-Devise Objectives & Strategies; (3) Re-Design Products & Services; (4) Re-Design DHS Operations; (5) Re-Design Resources & Organization. This model adopts a requirements-driven and capability-constrained approach using a top-down, bottom-up iterative process.[18] Vision and principles drive strategy and objectives, which drive products and services, which drive the operating concept needed, which places requirements on resources and organization. Conversely, capabilities of resources and organizations enable and constrain operations, which enable and constrain products and services, etc. The new DHS Strategic Plan includes results from the first three activities.[19]

A231, Re-Envision DHS & ID Principles.

The *Current Analyses & Predictions*, and *Change-Direction* including higher level vision, motives and inspiration, drive the re-work of *Vision & Principles of DHS*, constrained by *Strategic Capabilities* from A232.

A232, Re-Devise Objectives & Strategies.

Vision & Principles of DHS, Current Analyses & Predictions, and Change-Direction drive the re-design of DHS Objectives & Strategies, constrained by Product & Service Capabilities from A233.

A233, Re-Design Products & Services.

Enterprise Guidance (vision, principles, objectives, strategy) and *Current Analyses & Predictions* (including market research) drive the re-design of products and services, constrained by *Operational Capabilities* from A234, and guided by *Change-Direction* and relevant *Change Information & Recommendations*.

A234, Re-Design DHS Operations.

The DHS Operations Design is revised to deliver Products & Services Designs, consistent with Enterprise Guidance in responsive to Change-Direction. The activity considers Current Analyses & Predictions and Change Information & Recommendations, constrained by Resource & Organization Capabilities and Implementation Issues with Design.

A235, Re-Design Resources & Organization.

Resources and organization are re-designed to execute operations per the new *DHS Operations Design*, consistent with new *Enterprise Guidance*, in response to *Change-Direction* from management. This design activity considers *Current Analyses & Predictions* (including human capabilities and technology) and *Change Information & Recommendations*.

---

[18] An iterative re-design approach for complex systems is presented in Small and Downey 1998.

[19] *Securing our Homeland—U.S. DHS Strategic Plan*, February 24, 2004.

Table 8. A23 in Diagram Hierarchy

Diag.	Activity
A0	Operate & Change the Homeland Security Enterprise
A1	Operate Department of Homeland Security
A12	Provide & Maintain Resources
A122	Provide & Maintain Human Resources
A13	Accomplish the Priority Mission
A2	Change Department of Homeland Security
A23	Re-Design Department of Homeland Security
A235	Re-Design Resources & Organization

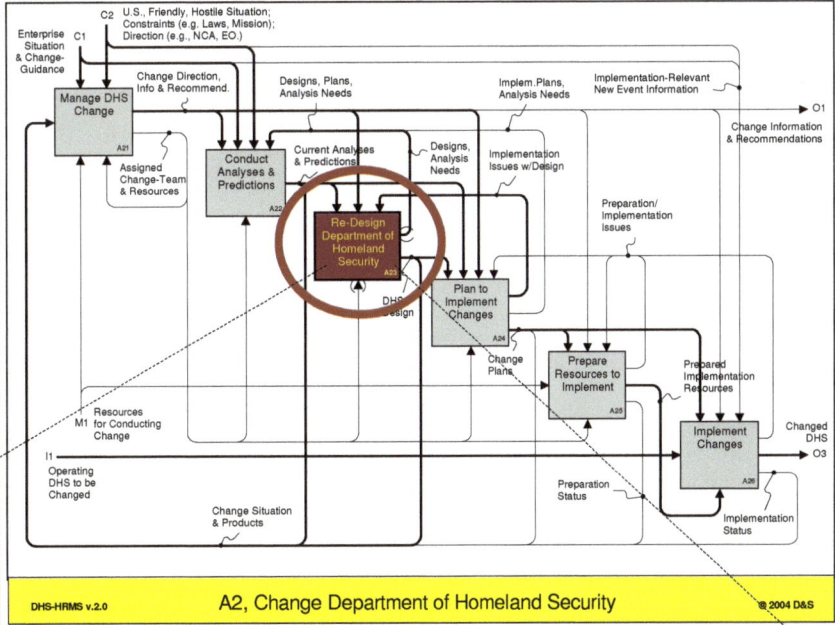

A2, Change Department of Homeland Security

DHS-HRMS v.2.0   © 2004 D&S

D&S SystemOps™ Model

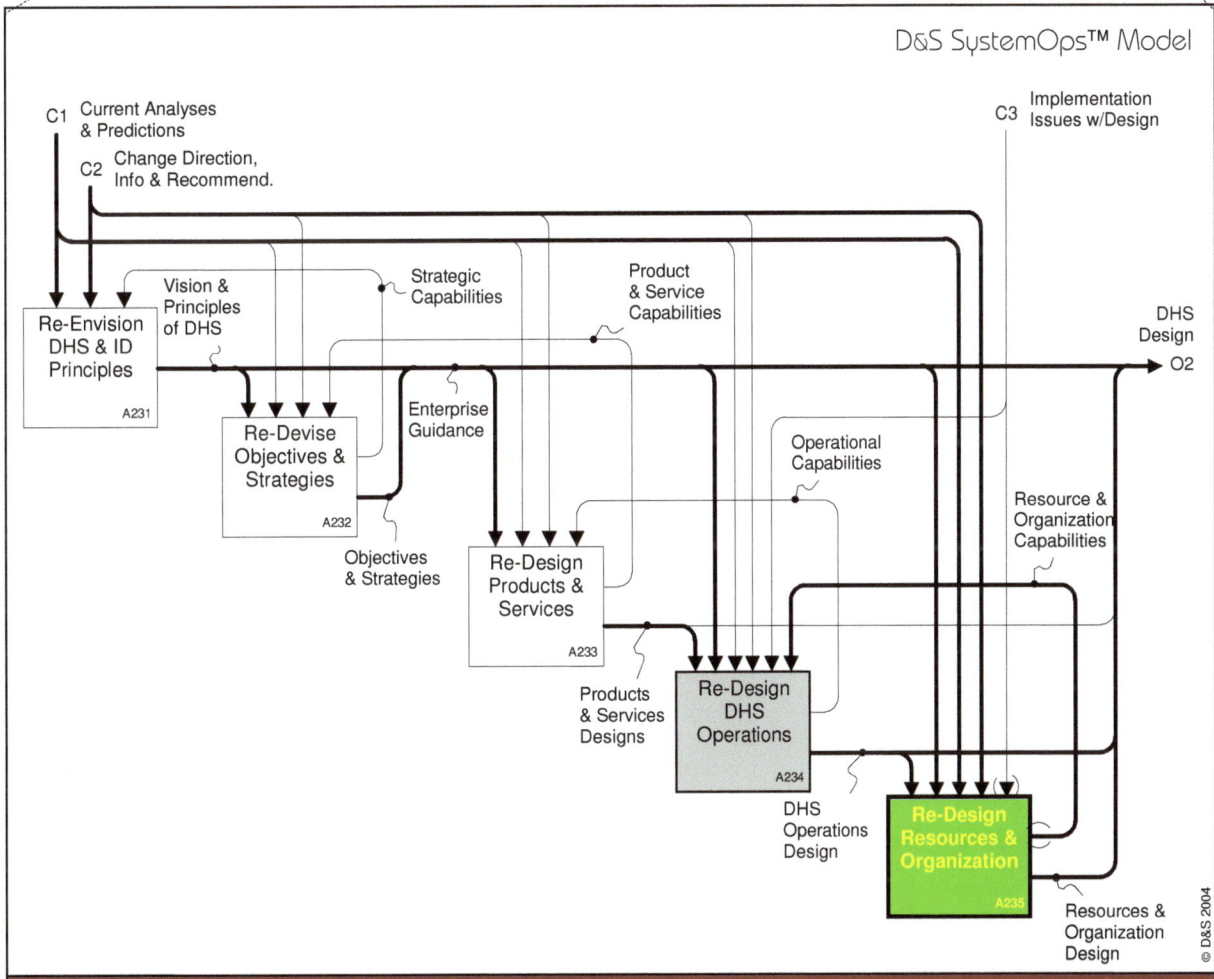

Diagram A23, Re-Design Department of Homeland Security   DHS-HRMS v.2.0

A235, Re-Design Resources & Organization

Resources and organization are re-designed to execute the *DHS Operations Design* consistent with *Enterprise Guidance*, in response to *Change-Direction*. This design activity considers *Current Analyses & Predictions* (including human capabilities and technology state-of-the-art) and *Change Information & Recommendations*, and may be constrained by *Implementation Issues with Design*.

Diagram A235 shows Re-Design Resources & Organization as five sub-activities: (1) Re-Specify Resources & Organization Requirements; (2) Re-Design Human Resources & System; (3) Re-Design Other Resources & Systems; (4) Re-Design Organization, Assignm'ts, and Mgt System; and, (5) Integrate & Evaluate Total Design.

A2351, Re-Specify Resources & Organization Requirements.

The *Operations Design* provides the basis for specifying *Resource and Organization Requirements*, and resolving resource integration issues. The many types of work for the DHS mission will require multiple talents and temperaments, as well as special management considerations.[20]

A2352, Re-Design Human Resources & System.

In response to Change-Direction and driven by the Human Resource Requirements and the DHS Operations Design along with DoD, CIA, FBI, etc. shown in A0.2, and considering Change Info & Recommendations and Current Analyses & Predictions, this activity produces specifications for the needed human resources, and a design for the system that provides those human resources. This activity does more than design an HRMS; it re-designs the human resources provisioning sub-enterprise. Its functionality is similar to A23; i.e., it revises the HR vision, objectives & strategies, products & services, operations concepts, and resources and organization. It works closely with the design for provisioning of related resources and makes design-adjustments to ensure integration.[21]

A2353, Re-Design Other Resources & Systems.

Other resources and systems are re-designed at the same time as HR, in response to *Other Resource Requirements* and in response to *Resource Provisioning System Needs for Other Resources*; e.g., computers for HR.

A2354, Re-Design Organization, Assignments & Management System.

Activities in DHS Operations Design are organized, the resources specified in resources designs are assigned to the organization, and the organizational management system is designed.

A2355, Integrate & Evaluate Total Design.

The re-design of all resource types must be sufficiently integrated to ensure compatibility among humans, equipment, and facilities so they work together as intended in the DHS Operations Design. Integration among the different specialties should start early in the design process to avoid lock-in of sub-optimized designs.

---

[20] For management of knowledge workers see Small & Downey-Small, 2008.

[21] At the Oct 2003 SRC meeting, Pete Smith commented on need to integrate SES management system with the HRMS.

Table 9. A235 in Diagram Hierarchy

Diag.	Activity
A0	Operate & Change the Homeland Security Enterprise
A1	Operate Department of Homeland Security
A12	Provide & Maintain Resources
A122	Provide & Maintain Human Resources
A13	Accomplish the Priority Mission
A2	Change Department of Homeland Security
A23	Re-Design Department of Homeland Security
A235	Re-Design Resources & Organization

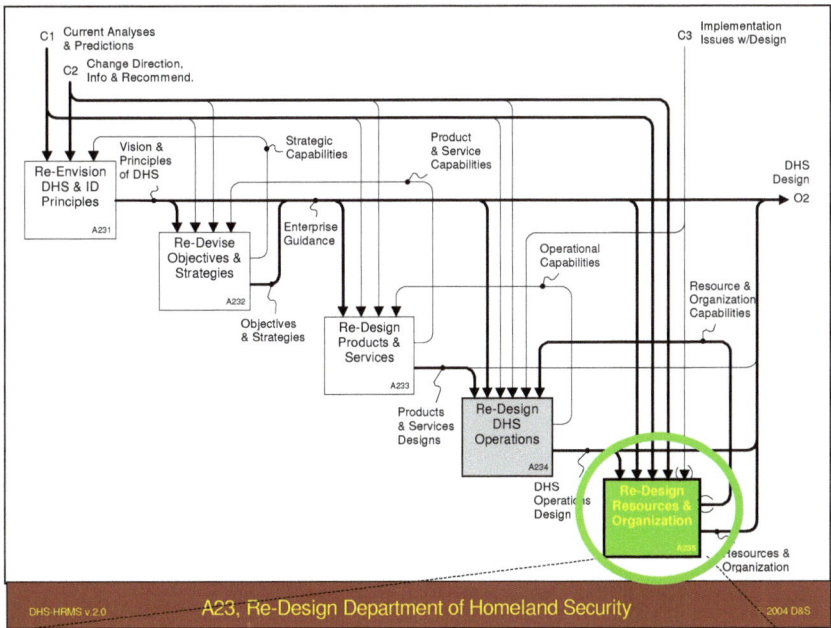

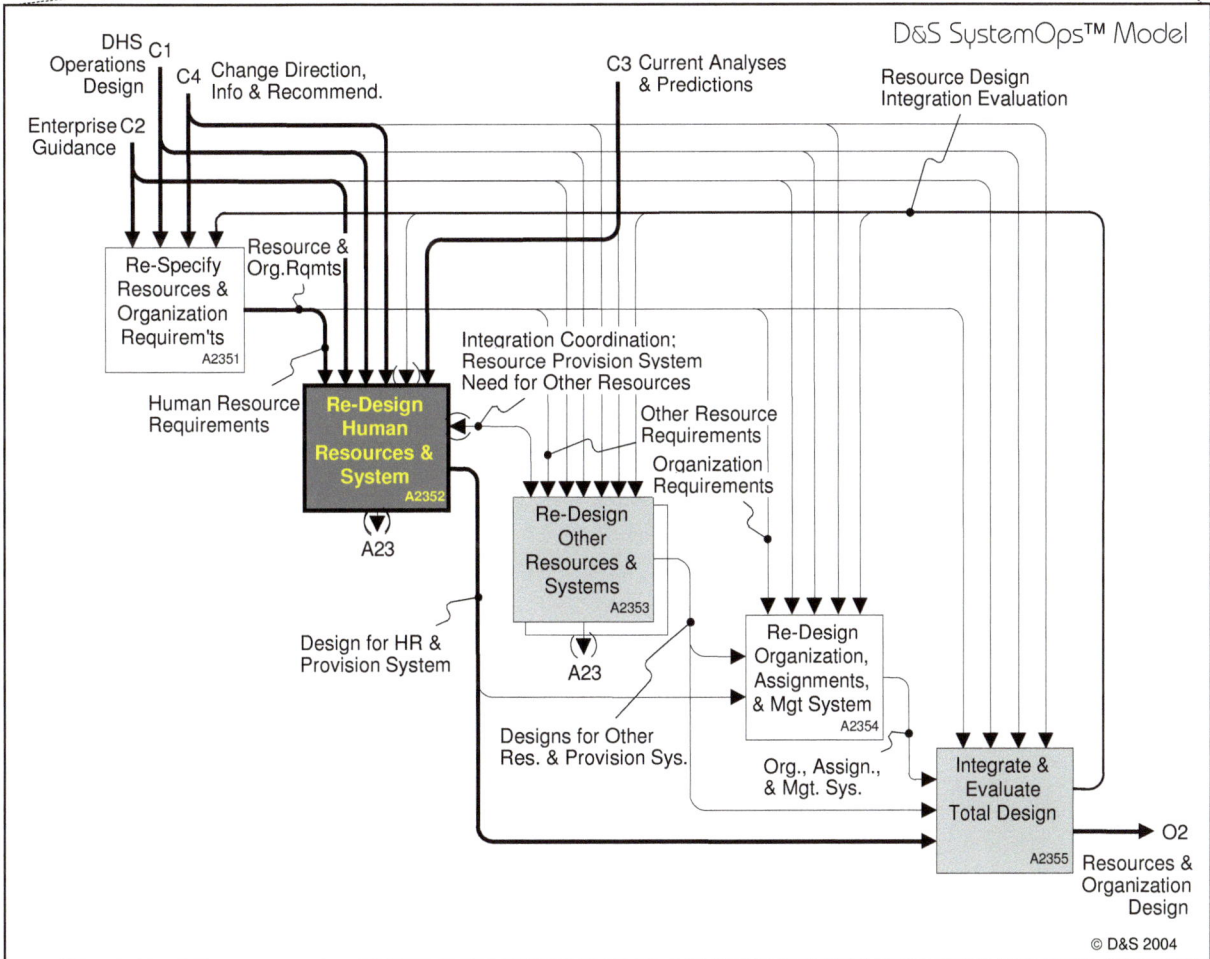

A23, Re-Design Department of Homeland Security

D&S SystemOps™ Model

Diagram A235, Re-Design Resources & Organization

DHS-HRMS v.2.0

© D&S 2004

III. HRMS Development

The preceding model portrays DHS operations and change activities and their key interdependencies. The model emphasizes development of a new Human Resources Management System (HRMS) in the context of DHS enterprise change, resources provisioning and mission operations.

This section uses the model from Section II[22] to present an approach for

DHS mission.[23]

The Mission is included in Constraints shown in Diagram A0 as a control on Operate DHS (A1) and Change DHS (A2). The Initial Enterprises & Resources for U.S. Homeland Security were the Operational DHS & Resources used to Operate DHS (A1) when DHS was stood up. Transition then began with Change DHS (A2) acting upon the

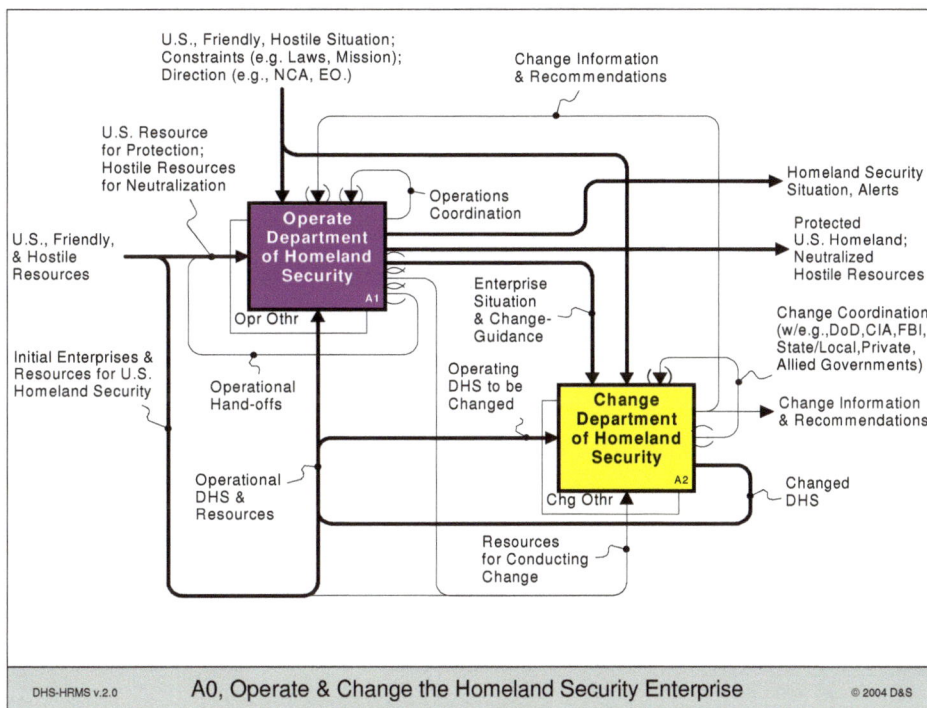

DHS-HRMS v.2.0 — A0, Operate & Change the Homeland Security Enterprise — © 2004 D&S

HRMS development, first looking at mission operations and required resources provisioning activities, then tracing the sequence of HRMS analysis, design, planning and implementation, as an integral part of the overall DHS change activities.

Starting Point

The DHS HRMS design starts with the

Operating DHS to be Changed.

The change activities are driven by the DHS mission, and the relevant current situations, friendly and hostile, external to and within the homeland security enterprise. Before examining the change activities (A2), we need to understand the DHS operations concepts (A1).

---

[22] Reduced diagrams from the model in Section II are repeated in this section for reference.

[23] Comment at Oct 2003 SRC meeting by Marta Perez, OPM

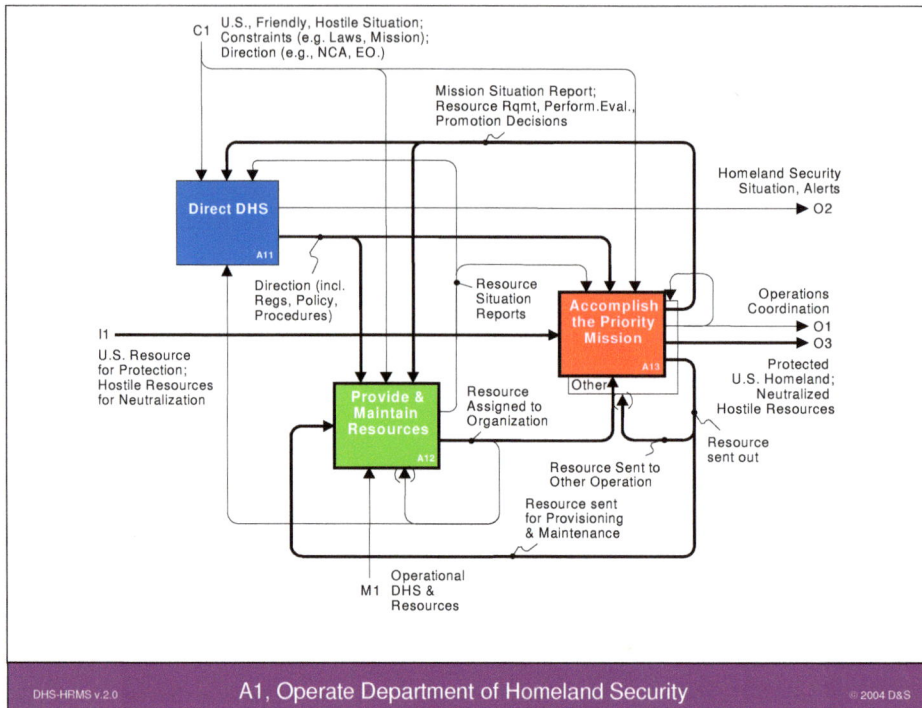

C1 U.S., Friendly, Hostile Situation;
Constraints (e.g. Laws, Mission);
Direction (e.g., NCA, EO.)

Mission Situation Report;
Resource Rqmt, Perform.Eval.,
Promotion Decisions

Homeland Security
Situation, Alerts
O2

Direct DHS
A11

Direction (incl.
Regs, Policy,
Procedures)

Resource
Situation
Reports

**Accomplish
the Priority
Mission**
A13

Operations
Coordination
O1
O3

I1

U.S. Resource
for Protection;
Hostile Resources
for Neutralization

Protected
U.S. Homeland;
Neutralized
Hostile Resources

**Provide &
Maintain
Resources**
A12

Resource
Assigned to
Organization

Other

Resource
sent out

Resource Sent to
Other Operation

Resource sent
for Provisioning
& Maintenance

M1 Operational
DHS &
Resources

DHS-HRMS v.2.0   **A1, Operate Department of Homeland Security**   © 2004 D&S

DHS Operations

The concept modeled in Diagram A1 shows DHS operations composed of three major interdependent activities— Direct DHS (A11), Provide & Maintain Resources (A12), and Accomplish the Priority Mission (A13).

The model contains descriptions of the generic activities within the resource provisioning activity (A12) and within the mission accomplishment activity (A13). The concepts for these two generic activities must be tailored for each DHS mission area. In each case, design of the concept for mission accomplishment must take precedence, supported by the resource provisioning concept design.

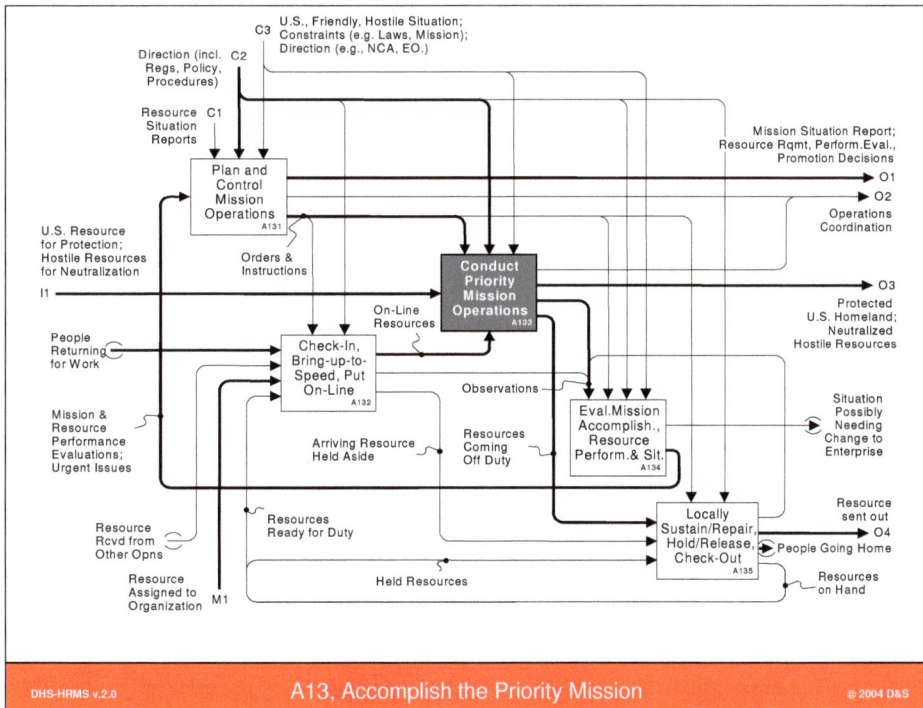

C3 U.S., Friendly, Hostile Situation; Constraints (e.g. Laws, Mission); Direction (e.g., NCA, EO.)

Direction (incl. C2 Regs, Policy, Procedures)

Resource C1 Situation Reports

Plan and Control Mission Operations A131

U.S. Resource for Protection; Hostile Resources for Neutralization

I1

Orders & Instructions

Conduct Priority Mission Operations A133

On-Line Resources

Mission Situation Report; Resource Rqmt, Perform.Eval., Promotion Decisions O1

O2

Operations Coordination

O3

Protected U.S. Homeland; Neutralized Hostile Resources

People Returning for Work

Check-In, Bring-up-to-Speed, Put On-Line A132

Mission & Resource Performance Evaluations; Urgent Issues

Arriving Resource Held Aside

Observations

Resources Coming Off Duty

Eval.Mission Accomplish., Resource Perform.& Sit. A134

Situation Possibly Needing Change to Enterprise

Resource Rcvd from Other Opns

Resources Ready for Duty

Locally Sustain/Repair, Hold/Release, Check-Out A135

Resource sent out O4

People Going Home

Resource Assigned to Organization M1

Held Resources

Resources on Hand

DHS-HRMS v.2.0 — A13, Accomplish the Priority Mission — © 2004 D&S

Mission Accomplishment

Diagram A13 displays a generic design for mission accomplishment. Several resource management activities are integrated within the mission accomplishment activity, because of their logical and temporal proximity to mission operations (A133). Therefore, these activities (A132, A134, A135) must be directly supervised and controlled by mission accomplishment managers.

The specifics of this concept depend upon the nature of the mission operations (in A133). The A13 model needs to be detailed and tailored for each DHS mission area, and for each resource category, including human resources. The tailored mission accomplishment concepts will drive, and be enabled and constrained by, the resource provisioning concepts (A12).

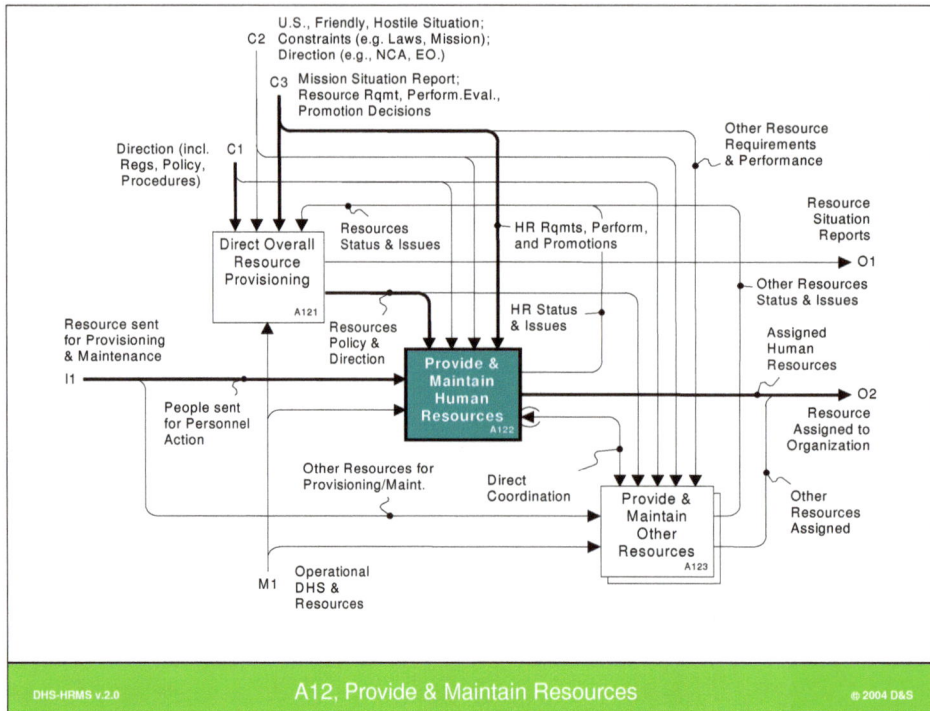

DHS-HRMS v.2.0   A12, Provide & Maintain Resources   © 2004 D&S

Resources Provisioning

Diagram A12 shows a generic overall resources provisioning and maintenance concept with key interfaces among provisioning direction (A121), and human resources (A122) and other provisioning (A123). A generic concept of operations for human resources provisioning & maintenance activities is shown in Diagram A122. These concepts should be tailored to support the operations concept for each mission area (per tailored A13 details).

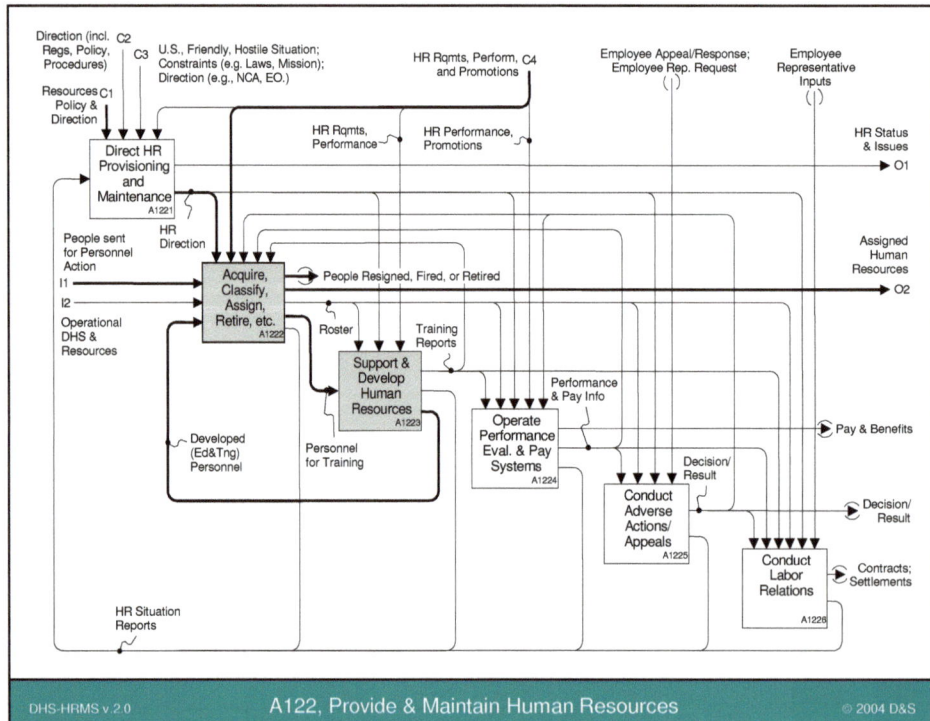

DHS-HRMS v.2.0   A122, Provide & Maintain Human Resources   © 2004 D&S

Diagram: DHS-HRMS v.2.0 — A2, Change Department of Homeland Security — © 2004 D&S

DHS Change

Design of the new operations concepts for DHS mission accomplishment and supporting resources provisioning (which includes the new DHS HRMS) is accomplished within the overall DHS change activity (A2).

Diagram A2 shows the change activities and their interdependencies involved in DHS change—at the beginning, during transition to DHS, and for continuing changes of DHS. The complexity of multiple change scenarios, some sequential, others simultaneous, and many overlapping, requires a change-framework and coordination.[24]

Emergency changes commenced September 11, 2001, followed by urgent near-term changes. When the Homeland Security Act of 2002 was signed, another set of changes began, including the "Transition" to DHS, which will be followed by continuing change as the situation demands.[25]

Basic Approach

First, the DHS Mission must be understood in order to Manage DHS Change (A21). The Mission and relevant situations are analyzed (A22) to determine the current situation and desired future situation, providing insight for re-design (A23). Transition from old to new design is planned (A24), preparations made (A25) and changes implemented (A26). [26]

Determining 'as-is'; Projecting 'to-be'

Conduct Analyses & Predictions (A22) studies the situations relevant to the mission. The scope is broad, including U.S., Friendly, and Hostile situations, present and historic. Regarding human resources, A22 should identify problems

---

[24] A framework for multiple changes is presented in Small and Downey, 1996.

[25] An integrated management approach for addressing multiple urgencies is presented in Small and Downey, 2001.
[26] At the Oct 2003 SRC meeting, Admiral Loy said due to the complexity of the subject we need to think of (a) what is broken with HR 'as is,' (b) the desired 'to-be,' and (c) the sequence, timeline and cost for how to get from (a) to (b).

with the existing systems in the context of the new DHS mission. During 2003 the SRC and HRMS Data Collection Team examined where we are and where we want to go. The information was used by the HRMS Design Team to develop options which were refined by the SRC and presented to DHS and OPM management in A21.

Using the A22 analysis and prediction results, A21 provides *Change-Direction* Design DHS Op'ns (A234) and Re-Design Resources & Organization (A235).

The 2004 DHS Strategic Plan contains the DHS vision, principles (A231), strategic goals and objectives (A232), and services (A233). The overarching framework being established for implementing the Strategic Plan as part of the *Future Years Homeland Security Plan* is intended to integrate strategy,

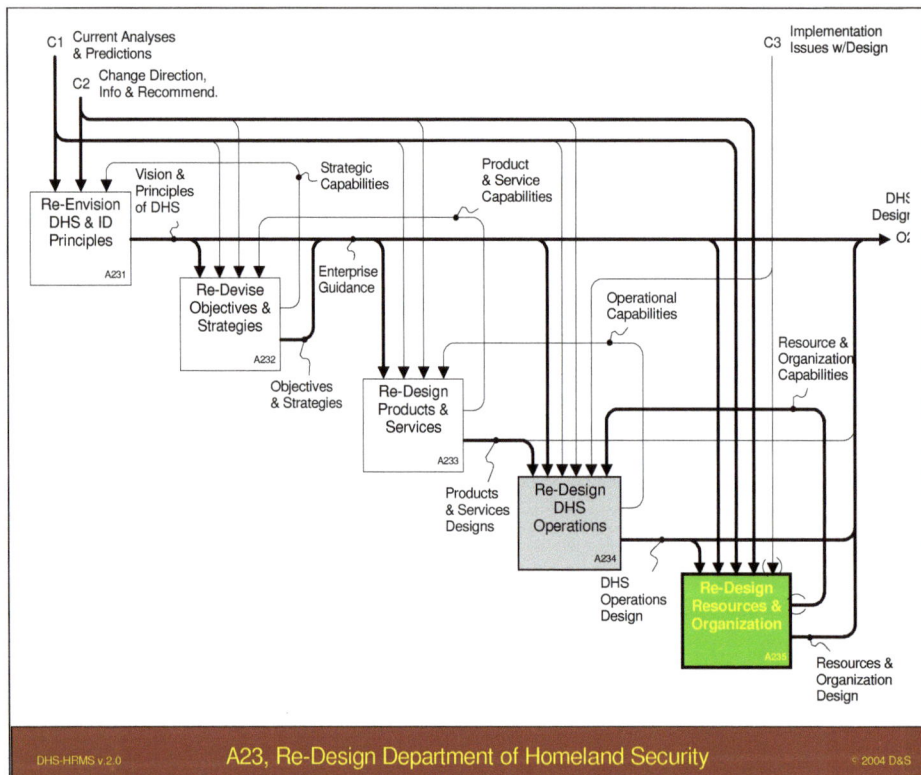

A23, Re-Design Department of Homeland Security

which guides the re-design in A23 of DHS, including the HRMS. As design proceeds, implementation issues identified in A24 are addressed by A23.

Designing What is Needed

Designing the new DHS, shown in Diagram A23, includes a "sequence" of interdependent activities—Re-Envision DHS & ID Principles (A231), Re-Devise Objectives & Strategies (A232), Re-Design Products & Services (A233), Re-

organizational structure, operations and culture with the DHS budget, thereby supporting its formulation.[27]

The first implementation priority of the Strategic Plan addressed mission fragmentation, omission and overlap. DHS operations concepts (in A133) must be designed (by A234) to provide for discrete mission areas, and frameworks

---

[27] *Securing our Homeland—U.S. DHS Strategic Plan*, February 24, 2004.

for interdepartmental coordination. Although operations concepts are implied by an organization chart, complex operations require explicit graphic design. DHS enterprise guidance and operations design then drive the design of resources and organization (by A235), including design of the DHS HR system (by A2352).[28]

The process may seem cumbersome for urgent situations. However, we believe need to revisit the entire set of re-design activities in successively greater detail.

For example, the 2004 DHS HRMS Proposed Rule appeared to contain mid-level detail.[29] We think implementation of any Final Rule requires refinement and clarification of the DHS operations design, which should be based upon corresponding DHS Strategic Plans.

Throughout the DHS re-design efforts in A23, close coordination with similar

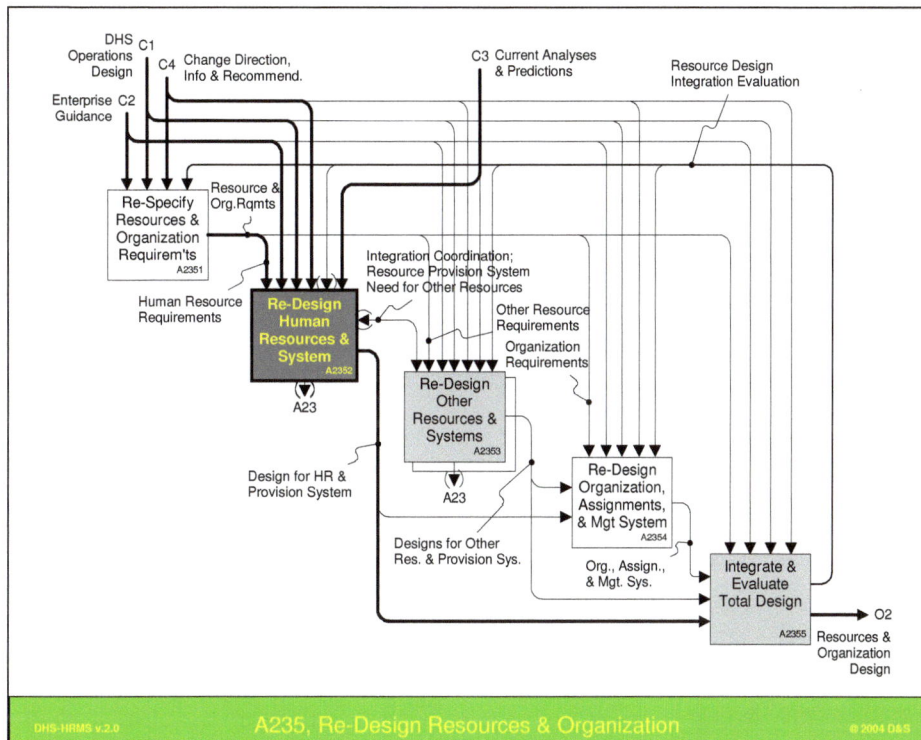

A235, Re-Design Resources & Organization

there was a high-speed effort to re-envision the enterprise, re-devise objectives & strategies, re-design products & services, and re-design operations, in order to re-design the resources and organization as defined in the Homeland Security Act of 2002. As the transition to the new DHS organization proceeds we anticipate a re-design activities in supporting enterprises (e.g., FBI, CIA, DoD, state and local governments) is essential. The visions, objectives and strategies must be consistent, the re-designed products and services complementary, and the operations interfaces coherent and effective.

---

[28] Major re-design of complex operations, resources and organizations, such as in the DHS transition, should be iterative (Small and Downey 1998)

[29] DHS HRMS Proposed Rule (5 CFR Chapter XCVII Part 9701), Federal Register, February 20, 2004; comments due March 22, 2004.

When operations depend upon one another for supporting or intermediate products, their design (by A234) must be done in concert and with sufficient detail to ensure cohesion. General statements of support, without explicit description, can result in significant disconnects.[30]

Planning How to Get There

After determining (a) the "as is" and (b)

The required changes in rules and their implementation plan are announced (by A21) in the Federal Register. Comments are considered and decisions made; any change in design/implementation required by a decision is accomplished (A23/A24) and approved (A21), and "final" regulations announced in the Federal Register (A21).

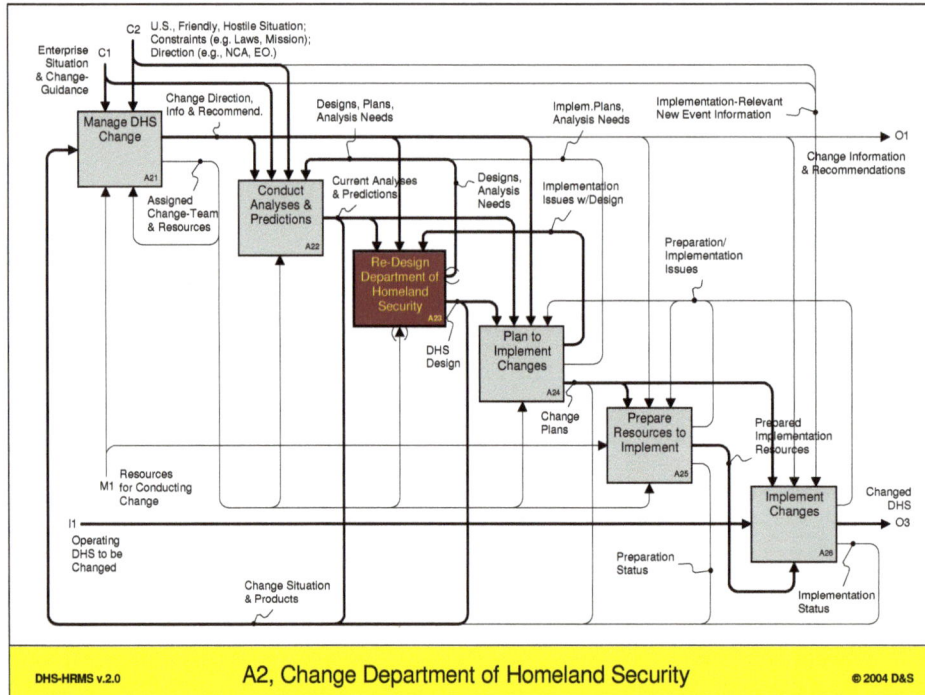

A2, Change Department of Homeland Security

the "to be" we can address Admiral Loy's third step, "How do we get from (a) to (b)?"

Referring again to Diagram A2, after analyses and prediction (A22) of the situation, and after a new HRMS and related enterprise services, operations concepts, and resources are designed (A23) and approved (A21), the implementation is planned (A24) and approved (A21).

Preparation & Implementation

The implementation resources are prepared in advance (in A25) and then used to implement the changes in the operating enterprise (in A26). A25 includes training of operations staff prior to change of operations; whereas on-the-job training (OJT) takes place in A26.

Numerous changes in DHS may be expected during the transition and beyond. Manage DHS Change (A21) is responsible for orchestrating all changes to ensure Implement Changes (A26)

---

[30] Executive Order 11490, FEMA Draft, 5 Jan 1982, described numerous government agency support relationships which were discovered to be inconsistent and uncoordinated. (Downey and Small, 1983)

generates a cohesive *Changed DHS* without disrupting DHS operations.[31]

Implementation Issues

Exceptional care is required in bringing a new HRMS on-line. Prototypes and test pilots should be considered for significant changes in operating concept. Conceptual prototypes may be developed and tested (in A23), production pilots may be tested off-line (in A25), and partial implementations may be installed, operated and evaluated (in A26) before widespread implementation.[32]

Planning a non-disruptive transition is vital for homeland security; gaps in coverage could be disastrous. Careful consideration of issues and preparation are essential (in A24, A25) to avoid problems during implementation (in A26). Further, the implementation activity (A26) must monitor the enterprise and environment for *Implementation-Relevant New Event Information*, before and after "switch-over," in order to delay or reverse the "switch-over" if the situation warrants.

---

[31] Full coordination is not always possible—external events may demand immediate response during a major transition. A change-model can enhance cohesion by highlighting critical coordination. (Small and Downey 1996)

[32] In the Oct 2003 SRC Meeting, Colleen Kelley, President, NTEU, was concerned about rushing to implementation; she also pointed out transition would require extra money. Pete Smith said it is very important to test options with employees to get feedback and rationale from multiple viewpoints.

IV. Conclusion

The historical assembly of 22 separate organizational units to create DHS with its vital mission to protect the Homeland from terrorist threat, was only the beginning of a continuing challenge for change.

The more successful DHS is in accomplishing its mission, the greater the risk of complacency, and the greater the need for sustained, consistent change leadership and management. Nowhere is this need greater than in Human Resources where a responsive, appropriately skilled and aligned workforce is dependent on a flexible, mission and performance based HRMS.

The preceding sections have presented a model of DHS Operations and Change, and a discussion of HRMS Development in relation to that model.

The authors built the model to provide a shared picture of the contextual framework for HRMS development, so that the rationale and requirements for HRMS components are clear, compelling and arguable. This presentation is made in the belief that a shared picture facilitates and improves communication and decision making. Accurate communication and consistent mission-focused decision making will be essential in developing and maintaining an HRMS which successfully supports the DHS mission--during an extended period of transition and change.

The model is both mission and human resources focused, portraying DHS operations to accomplish the mission, and resources (including human) supporting those operations. The Change activities are shown separately from the Operations to facilitate understanding of the change process. It is within the change process that the DHS operations and the supporting resource systems, including the HRMS, are redesigned and modified.

The model shows the close link between re-design of operations, and re-design of supporting resources. Looking at operations, the model depicts the dependency between accomplishing the mission and the resources support. The acquisition, training and development, evaluation and pay, and conduct of appeals and labor relations, are shown with relationships to mission situation and mission performance, and to the needs of the mission managers.

Proper design and implementation of DHS HRMS Rules will require refinement and clarification of the DHS operations design in each mission area of DHS. This refinement and clarification must be consistent with the current DHS Strategic Plan, and could benefit from graphic models of the mission operations concepts. Further, these graphic models could strengthen the overarching framework being established for implementing the current Strategic Plan as part of the Future Years Homeland Security Plan.

Epilogue

In the decade since 2001 we have been blessed to have no large-scale physical attack. But, it appears America is losing ground in the great spiritual war against evil, which places us squarely on the path to national disaster.

The number of leaders in business, government (legislature, executive and judiciary), education and media, who reject the God of the Bible and His laws, has reached the tipping point. When people, self-centered by nature, follow their own drifting moral compasses, they can eventually rationalize anything. Declining moral values carry over into institutions via individuals, diminishing the sense of responsibility and integrity, and the efficacy of oaths and professional codes of ethics.

The resulting evils of corruption and deceit endanger our national security and our constitutional republic. The government is not only failing to fulfill the purpose for which it was instituted—to secure all the "unalienable Rights" endowed by the Creator—but is actually violating some of those Rights. (See Small and Downey-Small 2010.) Further, the extensive unchartered government programs are bankrupting and weakening our nation.

We the People need to turn our hearts back to the Creator and reaffirm our exceptional national charter, the 1776 Declaration of Independence. America might then get back on course as the exceptional nation she once was, with a secure homeland.

We ask our fellow Americans to join in seeking God's Truth, obeying His will regardless of personal cost, and praying for His preservation of our republic. Psalm 127:1b cautions us, "Unless the Lord watches over the city, the watchman stays awake in vain." *

A. Small
E. Downey

Kensington, Maryland
Easter Monday, 2011

---

* Scripture quotation from *The Holy Bible, English Standard Version®*, copyright © 2001 by Crossway Bibles, a publishing ministry of Good News Publishers. Used by permission. All rights reserved.

Appendix

—

Graphic Modeling Language

Excerpt from D&S training material.
Copyright ©1993-2004, 2011, Downey & Small Associates, Inc. All right reserved.

Basic Notation

The graphic modeling language, IDEF$_0$, is used to visualize and improve processes.[33, 34] Boxes represent the activities of the process. Arrows represent things produced or used by the process; e.g., physical objects, information and data, people and organizations. The position an arrow enters a box has meaning: Arrows entering at left are "Inputs" representing things to be modified; at top are "Controls" representing information that influences the activity; at bottom are "Mechanisms" which are resources that perform the activity. Arrows departing at right are "Outputs" produced by the activity.

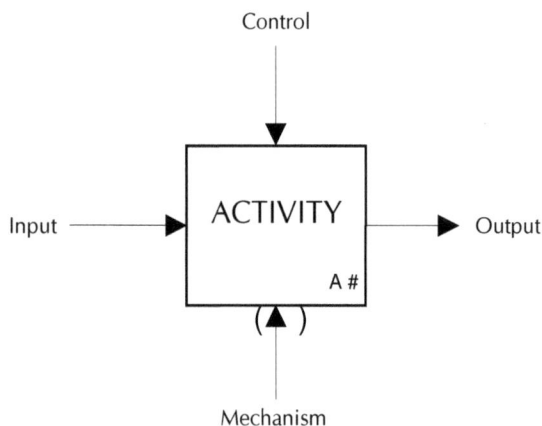

Control

Input → ACTIVITY → Output

A #

(▲)

Mechanism

Figure 2. Box & Arrow Syntax

An IDEF$_0$ diagram shows three to six activities (boxes) and their interdependencies (arrows). If a process needs more than six activities shown, the activities are grouped into a hierarchy of activities and sub-activities (called 'parents' and 'children').

Activities and sub-activities are assigned numbers corresponding to hierarchical position. A0 (A Zero) is the single overall activity performed by the process. The sub-activities of A0 are numbered A1, A2, ...; the sub-activities of A1 are numbered A11, A12, ...; and so on. The activity number is shown in the lower right corner of the box.

Diagrams are also assigned numbers. The diagram which shows the sub-activities (A1, A2, ...) of A0 is called the A0 diagram. The diagram which shows the sub-activities (A11, A12, ...) of A1 is called the A1 diagram. The diagram number is shown at the lower left of the diagram and is called the diagram node number.

In addition to the decomposition diagrams that show sub-activities and interdependencies within the process, there are context diagrams that portray the process interdependencies with external activities. The main context diagram of the model shows the A0 activity as a single box, and shows the key inputs, controls, outputs, and mechanisms. The main context diagram, numbered A-0 (A Minus Zero), is the focus of the model and defines its scope, purpose and viewpoint. The next higher level context diagram, numbered A-1 (A Minus One) shows the A0 and its most closely related external activities. Higher level context diagrams are numbered A-2, A-3, etc.

Parentheses on an arrow indicate the arrow is not visible on the next diagram in the hierarchy, although logically present. Such arrows are

---

[33] For formal description of IDEF$_0$ see FIPS Pub 183 (NIST 1993)
[34] IDEF$_0$ is based upon Structured Analysis and Design Technique developed by Doug Ross of MIT and SofTech (Ross 1977)

called 'tunnels' and are used to avoid clutter where their presence at the next level is obvious or unimportant to the purpose of the model. In the sample diagram at left, the mechanism arrow is 'tunneled' into the box and so will not be shown on a diagram that details the box.

Code numbers on arrows at the diagram border (e.g., 'C3' and 'O2') indicate the position that arrow enters or emerges from the corresponding box on the parent diagram (numbered from left to right, and top to bottom). Thus, 'C3' would be the third control from the left, and 'O2' the second output from the top. These codes provide local references only and are not globally unique.

Diagram Hierarchy

The IDEF$_0$ diagram hierarchy notation is shown in Figure 3. When referring to the hierarchy, the notation Axy refers to Diagram Axy but the notation Ax.y denotes box Axy on Diagram Ax. Both cases, Axy and Ax.y, represent the same Activity Axy. Diagram Axy shows the details of Axy while Ax.y shows the context of Axy within Ax.

A0 notation is similar; e.g., A0.2 denotes box A2 on Diagram A0, which represents Activity A2 whose details are shown in Diagram A2.

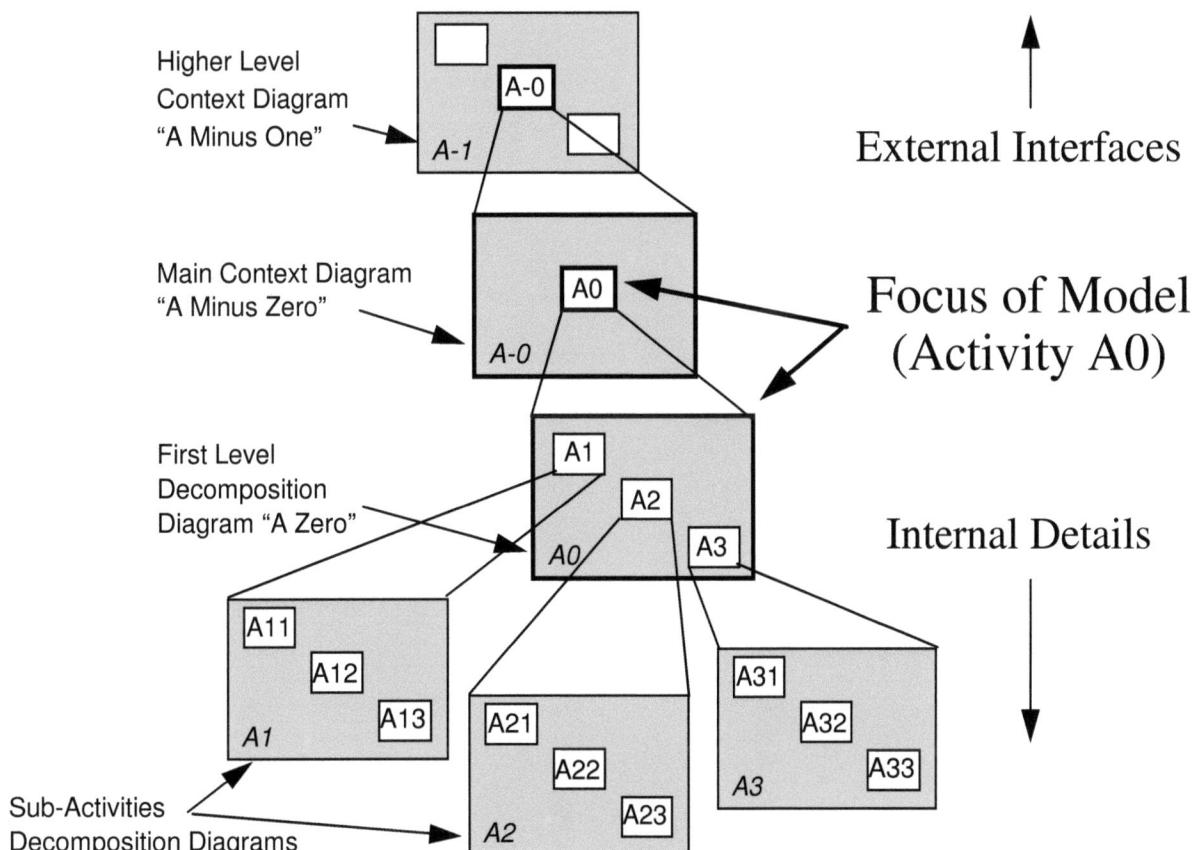

Figure 3. Diagram Numbering

Selected References

Downey, E. A. and A. W. Small. 1983. Preliminary emergency planning framework. Report, Downey & Small Associates, Inc. under contract EMW-C-1045 with Federal Emergency Management Agency, Washington.

National Institutes of Standards and Technology (NIST), U.S. Department of Commerce. 1993. *Integrated Definition for Functional Modeling (IDEF0)*. Federal Information Processing Standards Publication, FIPS Pub 183.

Ross, D. T. 1977. Structured Analysis (SA): a language for communicating ideas, *IEEE Transactions on Software Engineering*, SE3, 16—34.

Small, A. W. and E. A. Downey. 1996. Orchestrating multiple changes: a framework for managing concurrent changes of varied type and scope. *Proceedings, International Conference on Engineering and Technology Management, IEMC 96, 18-20 August, 1996, Vancouver, British Columbia.* 627—634. New York: Institute of Electrical and Electronics Engineers, Engineering Management Society.

— 1998. Re-designing enterprise operations, resources and organization. *Proceedings, International Conference on Engineering and Technology Management, IEMC 98, October 11-13, 1998, San Juan, Puerto Rico.* 387—396. New York: Institute of Electrical and Electronics Engineers, Engineering Management Society.

— 2001. Managing change: some important aspects. *Proceedings, International Engineering Management Conference, IEMC 2001, October 7-9, 2001, Albany, NY.* 50—57. New York: Institute of Electrical and Electronics Engineers, Engineering Management Society.

— 2005. Managing collection, analysis and prediction for enterprise change. *Proceedings, International Engineering Management Conference, IEMC 2005, September 11-14, 2005, St. John's, Newfoundland, Canada.* 349—353. New York: Institute of Electrical and Electronics Engineers, Engineering Management Society.

Small, A. W. and E. A. Downey-Small. 2008. Ancient wisdom for engineering managers: Drucker and Judeo-Christian concepts for managing creativity. *Proceedings, International Engineering Management Conference, IEMC 2007, Managing Creativity: The Rise of the Creative Class. July 29 – August 1, 2007, Austin, Texas, USA.* 49—53. New York: Institute of Electrical and Electronics Engineers, Engineering Management Society.

— 2010. The American national charter and concept of governance. *Proceedings, 2010 International Conference on Scientific and Social Research (CSSR), December 5-7, 2010, Kuala Lumpur, Malaysia.* 950—955. New York: Institute of Electrical and Electronics Engineers. Sponsored by the Research Management Institute, Universiti Teknologi MARA and Institute of Electrical and Electronics Engineers, Malaysia Section.

U.S. Marine Corps (USMC). 1994. The United States Marine Corps Combat Development Process, USMC CDP Version 1.1, 11 April 1994. Report, Downey & Small Associates, Inc. under sub contract SC-787-004 to Systems Research and Applications Corporation under prime contract MDA903-91-D-0061/D07, Department of Defense Corporate Information Management (CIM) Functional Process Improvement Program.

The Authors

Albert W. Small, born in Washington, D.C., received the B.S. and M.S. degrees in electrical engineering from the University of Maryland, College Park and the Ph.D. degree in aerospace engineering from the U.S. Air Force Institute of Technology, Dayton, Ohio.

Dr. Small managed systems engineering and business process improvement for 40 years. He is President of Downey & Small Associates, Inc., Kensington, Maryland, a management consulting and system engineering firm. He has led process analyses for GM, IBM, the U.S. Marines, NYSE, UBS, and Merrill Lynch. He was Director, Systems Integration, SRS Technologies-Washington. While serving in the U.S. Air Force he was Chief, Airborne Software Research, Air Force Avionics Laboratory, and Director, Computer Resources Development, Policy and Planning, Air Force Systems Command.

Elizabeth A. Downey, born in Leigh-on-Sea, Essex, England, received the B.A. degree in sociology with honors from the University of London, England, and a postgraduate certificate in social work from the University of Edinburgh, Scotland.

Ms Downey has 30 years experience in general management and consulting. She is Vice President of Downey & Small Associates, Inc., Kensington, Maryland, a management consulting and system engineering firm. She led analysis of emergency preparedness responsibilities of 33 Federal agencies for FEMA. She consulted to GM, the U.S. Marines, New York Stock Exchange, UBS, and Merrill Lynch, and participated in training courses for senior executives. She served on the Steering Committee of the Society for Enterprise Engineering.

Printed in U.S.A.

www.ingramcontent.com/pod-product-compliance
Lightning Source LLC
Chambersburg PA
CBHW060806270326
41927CB00002B/69